At Issue

Super PACs

Louise I. Gerdes, Book Editor

WITHDRAWN

GREENHAVEN PRESS
A part of Gale, Cengage Learning

GALE
CENGAGE Learning

Farmington Hills, Mich • San Francisco • New York • Waterville, Maine
Meriden, Conn • Mason, Ohio • Chicago

Elizabeth Des Chenes, *Director, Content Strategy*
Douglas Dentino, *Manager, New Product*

Articles in Greenhaven Press anthologies are often edited for length to meet page requirements. In addition, original titles of these works are changed to clearly present the main thesis and to explicitly indicate the author's opinion. Every effort is made to ensure that Greenhaven Press accurately reflects the original intent of the authors. Every effort has been made to trace the owners of copyrighted material.

Cover photograph copyright © Images.com/Corbis.

LIBRARY OF CONGRESS CATALOGING-IN-PUBLICATION DATA

Super PACs / Louise I. Gerdes, book editor.
    pages cm. -- (At issue)
    Summary: "Books in this anthology series focus a wide range of viewpoints onto a single controversial issue, providing in-depth discussions by leading advocates, a quick grounding in the issues, and a challenge to critical thinking skills"-- Provided by publisher.
    Includes bibliographical references and index.
    ISBN 978-0-7377-6864-0 (hardback) -- ISBN 978-0-7377-6865-7 (paperback)
    1. Campaign funds--United States--Juvenile literature. 2. Political action committees--United States--Juvenile literature. 3. Business and politics--United States--Juvenile literature. 4. Corporations--Political activity--United States--Juvenile literature. 5. United States--Politics and government--Juvenile literature. I. Gerdes, Louise I., 1953-, editor of compilation. II. Title.
    JK1991.S84 2013
    324'.40973--dc23
                                                        2013044038

Printed in the United States of America
1 2 3 4 5 6 7 18 17 16 15 14

Contents

Introduction

American voters trying to make decisions during congressional and presidential campaigns get plenty of advice from relentless ads funded by millions of dollars donated to independent groups not directly affiliated with the candidates. These organizations often mask the identities of donors and disguise their intentions with vague names, such as Americans for Prosperity, Workers' Voice, and Make Us Great Again, that evoke a positive identity. In the 2012 election, the political action committee (PAC) Restore Our Future spent more than $142 million dollars, 90 percent of which went to attack ads opposing Democratic candidates, primarily Barack Obama. In the same way, Priorities USA Action spent 100 percent of more than $66 million in donations on ads attacking Obama's opponent, Republican Mitt Romney. While donors cannot hide completely, they need not reveal their identity in the ads themselves. Voters must actually dig to find out who is funding the ads, sometimes seeking the help of watchdog groups. In addition, donors can spend as much money as they wish, as long as funds donated are made to organizations independent of candidate campaigns. Moreover, wealthy donors no longer have to create and disseminate political ads. They need only donate money to a PAC that will hire staff to do the work.

Although PACs are not new to politics, a series of court decisions have allowed for the creation of what many analysts are calling super PACs. Wealthy individuals have always been able to spend a significant amount of money influencing elections. How they spent that money, however, was strictly limited by campaign finance laws. In 1976, the US Supreme Court in *Buckley v. Valeo* held that private individuals can spend as much as they want on political ads, as long as the ads are not coordinated with a candidate and thus not a direct contribution, which remains strictly limited. The court in *Buckley* argued that money is speech and to restrict political ad spending would be to restrict that individual's speech. What the Supreme Court did in its 2010 *Citizens United v. Federal Election Commission (FEC)* decision was to allow the wealthy to pool their money with other donors and those donors could now include corporations and unions. However, individual contributions were limited to $5,000. Two months after the *Citizens United* decision, the DC Circuit Court of Appeals held in *SpeechNow.org v. FEC* that Congress could place no limits on PAC spending as long as PACs did not funnel that money to candidates. Thus was born the super PAC, whose donors need not reveal themselves in the primarily negative attack ads created by PACs. Immediately following the *Citizens United* decision, many analysts feared that the relative anonymity of corporate donations would corrupt political campaigns. Thus, one of several controversies reflective of the super PAC debate is whether, in the wake of *Citizens United*, Congress should increase the disclosure requirements of corporate political spending.

Some commentators claim that disclosure is part of the democratic process and helps voters. "Let's make sure the American people have a clear and accurate understanding of who's spending what to influence American politics," asserts Meredith McGehee, policy director of the Campaign Legal Center.[1] To achieve this goal while also recognizing that lawmakers would be unable to overturn a Supreme Court ruling, several Democratic members of Congress proposed legislation that would require strict disclosure requirements for PAC ads. The DISCLOSE Act (Democracy Is Strengthened by Casting Light on Spending in Elections) would require that like candidates, corporate executives appear in the ads produced by the PACs to which they donate. PACs also would be required to list their top five funding sources. According to Senator

1. Quoted in Kenneth Jost, "Campaign Finance Debates," *CQ Researcher*, May 28, 2010.

Charles E. Schumer (D-N.Y.), "In cases where corporations try to mask their activities through shadow groups, we drill down so that the ultimate funder of the expenditure is disclosed."[2] Although the 2010 DISCLOSE Act passed the House, it was blocked by Senate Republicans. The legislation has since been reintroduced, but many believe it unlikely to pass as long as Democrats are in the minority.

Enacting strict super PAC disclosure requirements, however, is not as partisan an issue as some claim. In truth, members of the Democratic party are not disclosure's only supporters. According to Chris Van Hollen, Maryland representative and former chairman of the Democratic Congressional Campaign Committee, "These are American values. Republicans, Democrats, independents recognize it's important to a healthy democracy."[3] Indeed, former Pennsylvania Governor Tom Ridge, a member of the Republican party, supports disclosure requirements. Since the Supreme Court will not allow financial limits on speech, Ridge maintains that Congress should tell candidates that "'any contribution in excess of $500 to $1,000 to you personally or the super PAC, it is on the Internet within 24 hours, so people can know.' Not quarterly. Transparency now, it is the best antiseptic."[4] This position supports the Republican view that corporate political spending should not be limited. Instead, many Republicans believe that the true antidote to campaign corruption is to reveal the money's source. "In a 21st century world, if anybody wants to give a candidate one million or two million dollars, give it. But I want every journalist, every opponent, every taxpayer, every citizen to know that that's who gave it," claims Ridge. Determining the purpose of the corporate donation is

2. Quoted in Jost, op. cit.
3. Quoted in Luke Rosiak, "Republicans Oppose Super PAC Disclosure," *Washington Times*, June 20, 2012.
4. Quoted in Sam Stein, "Super PAC Disclosure Requirements Hot Topic of Conversation Among GOP Candidates," *Huffington Post*, January 5, 2012.

then up to the voter. "They may draw no conclusions. They may draw the wrong conclusion. They may draw the right conclusion," Ridge reasons.[5]

Some analysts argue, however, that the DISCLOSE Act's requirements stifle speech because they discourage corporations from participating. Election law attorney Jan Witold Baran, argues that what he calls redundant, burdensome disclosure laws "suggest that the purpose of the redundancies and the burdens is not disclosure but to discourage speech."[6] Republican House Minority Leader John Boehner opposed the original legislation, arguing that in addition to violating free speech, the bill itself was a plan by the Democratic majority at the time to silence its opponents. The legislation, he maintains, led to back-room deals that, in turn, led to special interest exemptions. In a June 24, 2010, press release, Boehner claims that the act "allows the Humane Society to speak freely, but not the Farm Bureau. It would protect the AARP's rights, but not 60-Plus. And lastly it would protect the National Rifle Association but not the National Right to Life."[7] A law that restricts the speech of some and not others is a clear violation of the First Amendment, in Boehner's view. Not unlike DISCLOSE Act supporters, the act's critics also cross partisan lines. In fact, the American Civil Liberties Union (ACLU) opposed the act, claiming it "would inflict unnecessary damage to free speech rights and does not include the proper safeguards to protect Americans' privacy. The bill would severely impact donor anonymity, especially those donors who give to smaller and more controversial organizations."[8]

Others maintain that such requirements are unnecessary because corporations are not as likely to donate to super PACs

5. Ibid.
6. Quoted in Jost, op. cit.
7. John Boehner, "Dems' DISCLOSE Act Will Shred Our Constitution for Raw, Ugly, Partisan Gain," June 24, 2010. http://boehner.house.gov.
8. American Civil Liberties Union, "ACLU Urges No Vote on DISCLOSE ACT," July 26, 2010. https://www.aclu.org/free-speech/aclu-urges-no-vote-disclose-act.

as disclosure supporters claim. "Most people in corporate America are under more pressure not to engage in politics than they are to engage in politics," claims James Portnoy, chief counsel for corporate and government affairs at Kraft Foods and a former FEC official.[9] In truth, Kenneth Gross, an election lawyer who represents an array of large corporations, told Matt Bai of *The New York Times* in July 2012 that few of his clients had contributed to independent PACs early in the 2012 election year. According to Gross, some corporate leaders fear that these contributions might become public. These corporations hope to avoid the reaction that surrounded the Target department store chain in 2010, after it contributed $150,000 to a Minnesota group backing a conservative candidate opposing gay marriage. "If you've got a bank on every corner, if you've got stores in every strip mall, you don't want to be associated with a social cause," Gross concludes.[10]

Clearly, whether strict super PAC disclosure requirements are necessary to protect the political process from corruption or instead violate free speech remains hotly contested. The authors in *At Issue: Super PACs* debate these and other issues concerning the nature and scope of super PACs, their impact, and how best to regulate them. Whether super PACs will corrupt or improve political campaigns remains to be seen.

9. Quoted in Jost, Op. cit.
10. Quoted in Matt Bai, "How Much Has *Citizens United* Changed the Political Game?" *New York Times*, July 17, 2012.

1

The Assault of the Super PACs

John Nichols and Robert W. McChesney

John Nichols is Washington correspondent for The Nation, *a liberal national news magazine. Robert W. McChesney is a professor of communication at the University of Illinois. Nichols and McChesney are coauthors of* The Death and Life of American Journalism *and founders with Josh Silber of Free Press, of a media reform organization.*

The Citizens United *Supreme Court decision gave birth to super political action committees (PACs), funded by corporations, unions, and other groups that may engage in unlimited political spending independent of campaigns. Because they can easily shield the identity of contributors, super PACs corrupt the electoral process. Because politicians do not want the appearance of attacking their opponents, independent super PACS can deliver powerful negative messages. Indeed, super PACs spend heavily on negative political ads. Although these organizations legally must not collaborate with candidates, the lack of collaboration is an illusion. Unfortunately, the media profits from this negative political ad spending, which is more lucrative than unbiased journalism that helps voters understand the candidates and their views on the issues. The focus on negative ads also can turn voters away from the political process, further threatening democracy.*

We have seen the future of electoral politics flashing across the screens of local TV stations from Iowa to New Hampshire to South Carolina. Despite all the excitement about Facebook and Twitter, the critical election battles of 2012 and for some time to come will be fought in the commercial break on local network affiliates. This year [2012], according to a fresh report to investors from Needham and Company's industry analysts, television stations will reap as much as $5 billion—up from $2.8 billion in 2008—from a money-and-media election complex that plays a definitional role in our political discourse. As [Barack] Obama campaign adviser David Axelrod says, the cacophony of broadcast commercials remains "the nuclear weapon" of American politics.

The Citizens United *ruling and its Super PAC spawn have created a new revenue stream for media companies, and they are not about to turn the spigot off.*

We've known for some time that the pattern, extent and impact of political advertising would be transformed and supercharged by the Supreme Court's January 2010 *Citizens United* ruling. But the changes, even at this early stage of the 2012 campaign, have proven to be more dramatic and unsettling than all but the most fretful analysts had imagined.

Citizens United's easing of restrictions on corporate and individual spending, especially by organizations not under the control of candidates, has led to the proliferation of "Super PACs [political action committees]." These shadowy groups do not have to abide by the $2,500 limit on donations to actual campaigns, and they can easily avoid rules for reporting sources of contributions. For instance, Super PACs have established nonprofit arms that are permitted to shield contributors' identities as long as they spend no more than 50 percent of their money on electoral politics. So the identity of many, possibly most, contributors will never be known to the public, even though they are already playing a decisive role in the 2012 election season. Former White House political czar Karl Rove's Crossroads complex, for example, operates both a Super PAC and a nonprofit. And Rove's operation is being replicated almost daily by new political operations aiming their money at presidential, congressional, state and local elections. "In 2010, it was just training wheels, and those training wheels will come off in 2012," says Kenneth Goldstein, president of Kantar Media's Campaign Media Analysis Group. "There will be more, bigger groups spending, and not just on one side but on both sides."

The 2012 campaign has already confirmed that Super PACs are key players, more powerful in many ways than the campaigns waged by candidates and party committees. But don't expect commercial media outlets to shed much light on these secretive powers. Newsroom staffs have been cut, political reporting is down and local stations are too busy cashing in on what *TV Technology* magazine describes as "the political windfall." The *Citizens United* ruling and its Super PAC spawn have created a new revenue stream for media companies, and they are not about to turn the spigot off. "Voters are going to be inundated with more campaign advertising than ever," one investor service wrote in 2011. "While this may fray the already frazzled nerves of the American people, it is great news for media companies." Indeed, Super PAC ads allow stations to reap revenues from actual campaigns and from parallel "independent" campaigns targeting the same audience with different messages.

Here's what the next stage of American politics looks like on the screen: WHO, the NBC affiliate in Des Moines, was awash in political advertising the night before the Iowa caucuses. But some ads stood out. One of the most striking was a minute-long commercial featuring amber waves of grain fluttering in the summer breeze, children smiling and a fellow with great hair declaring, "The principles that have made this nation a great and powerful leader of the world have not lost their meaning. They never will." Then the guy with the great hair announced, "I'm Mitt Romney. I believe in America. And I am running for president of the United States."

Then came another ad, darker and more threatening, with grainy production values, old black-and-white photos and a blistering assault on the Republican presidential contender who had briefly leapt ahead of Romney in the polling: former House Speaker Newt Gingrich. "Newt has more baggage than the airlines," the ad warned, before linking Gingrich to "China's brutal one-child policy," "taxpayer funding of some abortions," "ethics violations" and "half-baked and not especially conservative ideals." Quoting a *National Review* poke at Gingrich, the ad closed with the line: "He appears unable to transform, or even govern, himself."

By the time the 2012 race formally began, . . . Super PACs had already logged $13.1 million in campaign spending . . . and most of it negative.

The first commercial is an old-school "closing argument" ad, all optimism and light, along with the usual campaign-season balderdash—the empty banalities of a front-running contender appealing to "principles" and a belief in America. The second represents another archetype: the no-holds-barred takedown of an opposing candidate, which politicians and their consultants traditionally avoid running on the eve of a big vote for fear of muddying their own message and appearing too negative. Romney's campaign paid for the "amber waves of grain" ad. But who was responsible for the "Newt Gingrich: Too Much Baggage" ad? Restore Our Future, a Super PAC that collected $30 million for the 2012 campaign—more than the combined spending of Lyndon Johnson and Barry Goldwater on the 1964 presidential campaign. And when Gingrich shot to the top of the polls a month before the

Iowa caucuses, the group steered $4 million into a TV ad campaign that knocked the former Speaker out of the lead and into a dismal fourth-place finish.

Who finished first in Iowa? And a week later in New Hampshire? The guy with the great hair and all the talk about "principles"—Mitt Romney. He also happened to be the guy who appeared before a dozen potential donors at the organizational meeting for Restore Our Future in July 2011. Romney's former chief campaign fundraiser moved over to Restore Our Future, as well as his former political director and other aides. Romney's old partner at Bain Capital helped Restore Our Future get off the ground with a $1 million check. Technically there can be no collaboration between Super PACs and the candidates they are supporting. But Timothy Egan of the *New York Times* stated the obvious: "This legalism of 'no coordination' is a filament-thin G-string. Everyone coordinates."

Gingrich complained about the presumably unethical and potentially illegal level of coordination between the "principled" Romney campaign and the thuggish Restore Our Future project. When Romney pled innocence and ignorance, Gingrich said: "He's not truthful about his PAC, which has his staff running it and his millionaire friends donating to it, although in secret. And the PAC itself is not truthful in its ads." But the griping didn't get him very far.

By the time the 2012 race formally began, on January 3, Super PACs had already logged $13.1 million in campaign spending in early caucus and primary states, most of it in Iowa and most of it negative. Romney, whose actual campaign spent only about one-third as much money on ads as did the Super PACs that supported him, emerged as the narrow winner. But he wasn't the only winner in Iowa or New Hampshire, where a similar scenario played out a week later. Local television stations like WHO in Des Moines and WMUR in Manchester cashed in, big-time, as would stations in later primary states. And station managers in battleground states across the country can hardly wait for the real rush, which will come when the Super PACs that have already been positioned to support the Republican nominee and Democrat Barack Obama spend their money in what is all but certain to be the first multibillion-dollar presidential race in history.

The total number of TV ads for House, Senate and gubernatorial candidates in 2010 was 2,870,000. This was a 250 percent increase over the number of TV ads aired in 2002, when the same mix of federal and state offices was up for grabs. Compared strictly with 2008, the amount spent on TV ads for House races in 2010 was up 54 percent, and the amount spent on Senate-race TV ads was up 71 percent. Even before this year's Iowa binge, it was clear that 2012 would see a quantum leap in spending from 2008, the greatest increase in American history, and most of this would go to TV ads. As Maribeth Papuga, who oversees local TV and radio purchases for the MediaVest Communications Group, says, "We're definitely going to see a big bump in spending in 2012."

Political advertising and elections are to TV what Christmas is to retail.

It's not as if Americans haven't already seen big bumps on what is becoming the permanent campaign trail. Consider how politics has changed in the past four decades. In 1972, a little-known Colorado Democrat, Floyd Haskell, spent $81,000 (roughly $440,000 in 2010 dollars) on television advertising for a campaign that unseated incumbent Republican US Senator Gordon Allott. The figure was dramatic enough to merit note in a *New York Times* article on Haskell's upset win. Fast-forward to the 2010 Senate race, when incumbent Colorado Democrat Michael Bennet defeated Republican Ken Buck. The total spent on that campaign in 2010 (the bulk of which went to television ads) topped $40 million, more than $30 million of which was spent by Super PAC-type groups answering only to their donors. In the last month of the election, negative ads ran nearly every minute of every day. The difference in spending, factoring in inflation, approached 100 to 1. The 2010 Colorado Senate race is generally held up by insiders as the bellwether for 2012 and beyond. As Tim Egan puts it, "This is your democracy on meth—the post-*Citizens United* world."

Local TV stations across the country have come to rely on the booms in political advertising that come during critical election contests. In the '70s, political ads were an almost imperceptible part of total TV ad revenues. By 1996, according to the National Association of Broadcasters (NAB), they had edged up to 1.2 percent. A decade later political advertising was approaching 8–10 percent of total TV ad revenue. For many stations, political advertising in 2012 could account for more than 20 percent of ad revenues, and in some key states far more than that. As former New Jersey Senator Bill Bradley put it, election campaigns "function as collection agencies for broadcasters. You simply transfer money from contributors to television stations."

Super PACs allow allies of candidates with the right connections . . . to pile up money that can then be used not to promote that candidate but to launch scorched-earth attacks on other candidates.

The 2010 election season saw record spending on broadcast advertising: as much as $2.8 billion. And that wasn't even a presidential election year. Wall Street stock analysts can barely contain themselves as they envision the growing cash flow. Eric Greenberg, a veteran broadcast-industry insider, says, "Political advertising and elections are to TV what Christmas is to retail."

Broadcasters aren't about to give away the present they have received from the Supreme Court. The NAB has a long history of lobbying to block any campaign finance reform that would decrease revenues for local television stations, such as the idea of compelling stations to provide free airtime to candidates as a public-service requirement. The NAB's prowess in Washington was summed up by former Colorado Representative Pat Schroeder, who said, "Their lobbying is so effective, they hardly have to flick an eyelash." After the *Citizens United* ruling, the NAB actively opposed key provisions of the DISCLOSE [Democracy Is Strengthened by Casting Light on Spending in Elections] Act, a measure supported by Congressional Democrats and a handful of reform-minded Republicans to roll back elements of the decision. But that's not all. The group has even opposed steps toward the transparency that Supreme Court justices who backed the *Citizens United* ruling agree is vital but that might shame (or at least expose) the excesses of Super PACs.

In Iowa, where the race was delayed by wrangling over the caucus date, there were fears the money would not flow. But once the timeline was set, WHO, the NBC affiliate, along with another Des Moines station, took in nearly $3.5 million in the last weeks of 2011. A local station manager admitted he was prepared to interrupt his New Year's Eve dinner to upload new political ads. In all, more than $12.5 million worth of advertising was purchased in the Iowa race, and December 2011 revenues for WHO were up more than 50 percent from December 2010. The driver in the frenzy of last-minute TV advertising in Iowa and New Hampshire was the Super PACs.

Super PAC advertising is not like traditional campaign advertising. As the scenario that played out in Iowa illustrates, Super PACs allow allies of candidates with the right connections to the right CEOs and hedge-fund managers to pile up money that can then be used not to promote that candidate but to launch scorched-earth attacks on other candidates. The scenario is particularly well suited to negative advertising. This warps the process in a perverse way, creating a circumstance where a candidate who is not particularly appealing to voters but who *is* particularly appealing to a small group of 1 percenters can, with the help of well-funded friends, frame a campaign in his favor.

The threat to democracy plays out on a number of levels. Candidates without the right connections may prevail in traditional tests—as Gingrich did with strong debate performances and Rick Santorum did with grassroots organizing and a solid finish in Iowa. But they are eventually targeted and taken out by the Super PACs, and the candidate with the right connections, in this case Romney, enjoys smooth sailing. In Iowa, roughly 45 percent of all ads aired on local TV stations: thousands of commercials, one after another, attacking Gingrich.

Negative advertising can be effective even if it does not generate a single new voter for the candidate favored by the Super PAC placing the ad. If negative ads simply scare off potential backers of an opponent, that's a victory. Moreover, negative ads often force targeted candidates to respond to charges, no matter how spurious. And our lazy and underresourced news media allow the ads to set the agenda for coverage, thereby magnifying their importance and effect.

The main consequence of negative ads is that they demobilize citizens and turn them away from electoral politics.

The most comprehensive research to date concludes that between 2000 and 2008 the overall percentage of political TV ads that were negative increased from 50 percent to 60 percent. And 2008 is already beginning to look like a tea party. The percentage and number of attack ads in 2010 were "unprecedented," and they are increasing sharply again in 2012.

"I just hate it, and there's so much of it," Sarah Hoffman complained to a reporter at a Gingrich event in the Iowa town of Shenandoah. "Anytime they do anything negative, I just turn it off." Gingrich emerged as a born-again reformer for about ninety-six hours during his Iowa free-fall, telling voters like Hoffman: "It will be interesting to see whether, in fact, the people of Iowa decide that they don't like the people who run negative ads, because you could send a tremendous signal to the country that the era of nasty and negative thirty-second campaigns is over."

If a signal was sent from Iowa, it was that many voters would rather switch off than try to sort out the attacks. With no competition on the Democratic side, and with conservatives supposedly all ginned up to choose a challenger for President Obama, Republicans confidently suggested that caucus turnout would rise from 119,000 in 2008 to as much as 150,000 in 2012. Instead, turnout was up only marginally, to around 122,000. If the maverick candidacy of Ron Paul had not attracted thousands of new voters to the caucuses—many of them antiwar and pro-civil liberties independents unlikely to vote Republican in the fall—the turnout would almost certainly have fallen to pre-2008 levels. "If all people hear are negatives, a lot of them are just going to ask, Why bother?" says Ed Fallon, a former Democratic legislator and local radio host in Des Moines who caucused this year as a Republican. "And they're even more frustrated by the fact that the money for the negative campaigning comes from all these unidentified sources on Wall Street."

The research of scholars Stephen Ansolabehere and Shanto Iyengar demonstrates that the main consequence of negative ads is that they demobilize citizens and turn them away from electoral politics. This fact is a "tacit assumption among political consultants," they explain, arguing that the trend is toward "a political implosion of apathy and withdrawal."

Were national and local broadcast media outlets to cover politics as anything more than a horse race and a clash of personalities, they might be able to undo much of the damage. But stations across the country—and the newspapers they often depend on for serious coverage—have eviscerated local reporting in recent years. Surveys suggest that news programs now devote far less time to political coverage than they did twenty or thirty years ago. To the extent that campaigns are covered, the focus is on personalities and the catfight character of the competition. So it was that when Gingrich complained about the battering he was taking from the Super PACs, the story was portrayed as a dust-up between a pair of candidates rather than as evidence of a structural crisis. In part, this is the fault of the candidates, who for the most part do not want to speak too broadly about Super PAC abuses in which they are engaging or in which they hope to engage.

[Campaign] coverage is cheap and easy to do, and lends itself to gossip and endless chatter, even as it sometimes provides the illusion that serious affairs of state are under scrutiny.

Once it became clear that the media had no real interest in examining the problem, Gingrich quickly got with the program. Rather than make an issue out of campaign corruption, Gingrich's own Super PAC, Winning Our Future, corralled a $5 million donation from the spare-change drawer of Las Vegas casino mogul Sheldon Adelson (listed by *Forbes* as the eighth-wealthiest American, with a $21 billion fortune) just before the New Hampshire primary. The plan was to launch a blitzkrieg against Romney. Here we finally get the proper metaphor for post-*Citizens United* elections: mutually assured destruction, with citizens and the governing process the only certain casualties.

Unfortunately, the media outlets that could challenge this doomsday scenario tend to facilitate it. The elimination of campaign coverage is masked to a certain extent because the gutting of newsrooms also encourages what sociologist Herbert Gans describes as the conversion of political news into campaign coverage. As campaigns have become permanent, so has campaign coverage. Such coverage is cheap and easy to do, and lends itself to gossip and endless chatter, even as it sometimes provides the illusion that serious affairs of state are under scrutiny. To someone watching cable news channels, it might seem that presidential races have never been so thoroughly exhumed by reporters. But the coverage is as nutrition-free as a fast-food hamburger. After a panel of "experts" finish "making sense" of Rick Perry's debate performances, political ads don't look so bad.

With the little news coverage that remains focusing overwhelmingly on the presidential race, Congressional, statewide and local races get little attention nationally or even locally. Not surprisingly, research suggests that political TV advertising is even more effective further down the food chain. "In presidential campaigns, voters may be influenced by news coverage, debates or objective economic or international events," the Brookings Institution's Darrell West explained in 2010. "These other forces restrain the power of advertisements and empower a variety of alternative forces. In Congressional contests, some of these constraining factors are absent, making advertisements potentially more important. If candidates have the money to advertise in a Congressional contest, it can be a very powerful force for electoral success."

West's point is confirmed by a simple statistic from the 2010 races: of fifty-three competitive House districts where Rove and his compatriots backed Republicans with "independent" expenditures that easily exceeded similar expenditures made on behalf of Democrats—often by more than $1 million per district, according to [citizen advocacy group] Public Citizen—Republicans won fifty-one.

To the extent that media outlets cover campaigns, they highlight the "charge and countercharge" character of the fight as an asinine personality clash between candidates. But the real clash is between money and democracy. And the media outlets that continue to play a critical role in defining our discourse are not objecting. They are cashing in. Meanwhile, citizens are checking out.

2

Super PACs Weaken the US Political System

Ralph Nader

Ralph Nader, a former presidential candidate, is an attorney, author, and political activist known for his interest in consumer protection, humanitarianism, environmentalism, and democratic government.

Super political action committees (PACs) unduly influence America's political system by giving corporations more power. The Citizens United *Supreme Court decision allows corporate leaders to donate unlimited money to cast in a negative light politicians they oppose without consulting the company's stockholders. Corporations already exert influence over the US Congress through huge lobbying budgets. Nevertheless, a majority of the Supreme Court did not take into consideration the power of super PACS to influence Congress and drown out the voice of citizen voters. The court's dissent argued that the US Constitution does not grant corporations the same rights as individuals. Indeed, the founders recognized the need to curtail the power of corporations. Because the decision is the law of the land, however, only a constitutional amendment will effectively counter the power of the super PACs.*

Yesterday's [January 21, 2010] 5-4 decision by the U.S. Supreme Court in *Citizens United v. Federal Election Commission* shreds the fabric of our already weakened democracy by allowing corporations to more completely dominate our corrupted electoral process. It is outrageous that corporations already attempt to influence or bribe our political candidates through their political action committees (PACs), which solicit employees and shareholders for donations.

With this decision, corporations can now directly pour vast amounts of corporate money, through independent expenditures, into the electoral swamp already flooded with corporate campaign PAC contribution dollars. Without approval from their shareholders, corporations can reward or intimidate people running for office at the local, state, and national levels.

A Fantasy World

Much of this 183 page opinion requires readers to enter into a fantasy world and accept the twisted logic of Justice [Anthony] Kennedy, who delivered the opinion of the Court, joined by Chief Justice [John G.] Roberts, and Justices [Antonin] Scalia, [Samuel] Alito, and [Clarence] Thomas. Imagine the majority saying the "Government may not suppress political speech based on the speaker's corporate identity."

Perhaps Justice Kennedy didn't hear that the financial sector invested more than $5 billion in political influence purchasing in Washington over the past decade, with as many as 3,000 lobbyists winning deregulation and other policy decisions that led directly to the current financial collapse, according to a 231-page report titled: "Sold Out: How Wall Street and Washington Betrayed America."

The Center for Responsive Politics reported that last year the U.S. Chamber of Commerce spent $144 million to influence Congress and state legislatures.

The Center also reported big lobbying expenditures by the Pharmaceutical Research and Manufacturers of America (PhRMA) which spent $26 million in 2009. Drug companies like Pfizer, Amgen and Eli Lilly also poured tens of millions of dollars into federal lobbying in 2009. The health insurance industry trade group America's Health Insurance Plans (AHIP) also spent several million lobbying Congress. No wonder Single Payer Health insurance—supported by the majority of people, doctors, and nurses—isn't moving in Congress.

The Court's ruling threatens to undermine the integrity of elected institutions across the Nation.

Energy companies like ExxonMobil and Chevron are also big spenders. No wonder we have a national energy policy that is pro-fossil fuel and that does little to advance renewable energy.

No wonder we have the best Congress money can buy.

I suppose Justice Kennedy thinks corporations that overwhelm members of Congress with campaign contributions need to have still more influence in the electoral arena. Spending millions to lobby Congress and making substantial PAC contributions just isn't enough for a majority of the Supreme Court. The dictate by the five activist Justices was too much for even Republican Senator John McCain, who commented that he was troubled by their "extreme naivete."

A Touch of Reality

There is a glimmer of hope and a touch of reality in yesterday's Supreme Court decision. Unfortunately it is the powerful 90 page dissent in this case by Justice [John P.] Stevens joined by Justices [Ruth Bader] Ginsburg, [Stephen] Breyer, and [Sonia] Sotomayor. Justice Stevens recognizes the power corporations wield in our political economy. Justice Stevens finds it "absurd to think that the First Amendment prohibits legislatures from taking into account the corporate identity of a sponsor of electoral advocacy." He flatly declares that, "The Court's ruling threatens to undermine the integrity of elected institutions across the Nation."

He notes that the Framers of our Constitution "had little trouble distinguishing corporations from human beings, and when they constitutionalized the right to free speech in the First Amendment, it was the free speech of individual Americans that they had in mind." Right he is, for the words "corporation" or "company" do not exist in our Constitution.

Justice Stevens concludes his dissent as follows:

> "At bottom, the Court's opinion is thus a rejection of the common sense of the American people, who have recognized a need to prevent corporations from undermining self government since the founding, and who have fought against the distinctive corrupting potential of corporate electioneering since the days of Theodore Roosevelt. It is a strange time to repudiate that common sense. While American democracy is imperfect, few outside the majority of this Court would have thought its flaws included a dearth of corporate money in politics."

It is time to prevent corporate campaign contributions from commercializing our elections and drowning out the voices and values of citizens and voters.

Restoring the Sovereignty of the People

Indeed, this corporatist, anti-voter majority decision is so extreme that it should galvanize a grassroots effort to enact a simple Constitutional amendment to once and for all end corporate personhood and curtail the corrosive impact of big money on politics. It is time to prevent corporate campaign contributions from commercializing our elections and drowning out the voices and values of citizens and voters. It is way overdue to overthrow "King Corporation" and restore the sovereignty of "We the People"! Remember that corporations, chartered by the state, are our servants, not our masters.

Legislation sponsored by Senator Richard Durbin (D-IL) and Representative John Larson (D-CT) would encourage unlimited small-dollar donations from individuals and provide candidates with public funding in exchange for refusing corporate contributions or private contributions of more than $100.[1]

It is also time for shareholder resolutions, company by company, directing the corporate boards of directors to pledge not to use company money to directly favor or oppose candidates for public office.

1. The Fair Elections Now Act was introduced in 2010 and reintroduced in 2011. Analysts generally agree it has little chance of ever becoming law in the near future.

3

Have Faith in the American Voter

Trevor Burrus

Trevor Burrus is a research fellow at the Cato Institute, a libertarian think tank. At Cato's Center for Constitutional Studies, he studies constitutional law, civil and criminal law, legal and political philosophy, and legal history.

Those who are concerned about divisive politics often blame campaign spending. However, political advertising does not brainwash American voters, who are savvier than critics believe. Money that corporations, unions, or other groups donate to super political action committees (PACs) creates more speech, not less. Although super PAC ads sometimes may be misleading or even inaccurate, American voters know this strategy. Moreover, these ads will not influence those who already have strong political views. Provocative super PAC ads inspire political debate and might motivate undecided voters to look further into outrageous claims. Thus, efforts to regulate super PAC speech underestimate the American voter and actually mute the political process.

Are American voters savvy and competent political consumers or are they like children, getting spoon-fed flashy commercials for sugary cereal during Saturday morning cartoons? After all, commercials aimed at kids are regulated on the theory that children are not competent enough to resist ads. Is this how we should treat American adults when it comes to political ads?

Trevor Burrus, "Have Faith in the American Voter," *New York Daily News*, October 22, 2012. Copyright © Daily News, L.P. (New York). Used with permission.

The debate over campaign spending would change drastically if we believed in the competence of our fellow Americans. Competent people watch campaign ads with a suitable amount of skepticism and curiosity. Incompetent people, however, sit back and allow their opinions to be manipulated by flashy hokum.

Unfortunately, because of our increasingly party-segmented world—Republicans only know Republicans and only get news and opinions from Republican sources, and vice versa—Americans are more likely to believe that half of their countrymen are not just wrong, but that they're completely out of their minds.

What, exactly, is causing half of Americans to have insane political opinions?

Campaign spending has become the explanation for far too many: Secretive forces are spending vast amounts of "dark money" in an effort to brainwash Americans—and it's worked on 50% of us. Of course, which 50% depends on where you stand.

If you believe in the competence of Americans, and that rational, informed people can disagree with you, then [some misleading or inaccurate speech] should not be a problem.

But informed Americans can be either Republicans or Democrats, and no sinister explanation is needed. Nor are we simply clay in the hands of political ad-makers.

Moreover, this view of campaign spending ignores the value of free speech in the political sphere.

Money given to campaigns, super PACs or spent independently by individuals or corporations creates more speech. The Supreme Court in its *Citizens United* ruling—which allowed corporations to fund political speech that is independent of campaigns—increased the amount of political speech during the election season.

Some of that speech may be misleading or inaccurate, but if you believe in the competence of Americans, and that rational, informed people can disagree with you, then this should not be a problem.

Studies also show that political ads can persuade, as the best have done ever since Lyndon B. Johnson's 1964 "Daisy" ad.[1] Persuasion is, after all, the whole point. Yet persuasion is not the same as brainwashing, even when someone is persuaded to believe something you regard as fundamentally wrong, if not outright dangerous.

Of course, the ads are expectedly political—heavy on rhetoric, and relatively light on substance—but Americans know this. Political speech is like any other form of advertising, and Americans, flooded as they are with advertisements of all kinds, thus already know to take political advertisement with a grain of salt.

Political ads have little to no effect on the ideologically committed. A life-long Democrat will assume a [Republican Mitt] Romney-[Paul] Ryan ad is making misleading and inaccurate claims, and a committed Republican will think the same about ads supporting President Obama.

If an ad makes a strong, provocative claim, these voters might become motivated to research the issue further and make a more informed decision about whom to vote for.

Both partisans will roll their eyes and ask, "Who would be convinced by this stuff?" They will then imagine that hypothetical person, someone hypnotized by campaign rhetoric and beguiled by mellifluous narrators.

---

1. A 1964 presidential campaign ad that juxtaposed a young girl counting daisy petals with a countdown to a nuclear missile launch. Although the ad only aired once, it is believed to have been a contributing factor in Lyndon Johnson's landslide victory over Republican Barry Goldwater.

"Before *Citizens United*," the partisans will think, "those people were protected from this kind of misleading political speech that they are intellectually unprepared to hear."

Those voters who were "protected" from campaign ads before *Citizens United* were generally nonpartisan and not politically involved. Rather than being hypnotized by campaign rhetoric, these voters would have typically ignored it.

Today, if an ad makes a strong, provocative claim, these voters might become motivated to research the issue further and make a more informed decision about whom to vote for. Studies show that political ads increase both voter engagement and knowledge.

Strong ads are often criticized for "negative" messages that sully politics. But forceful, critical political speech works—it informs, it excites and causes people to perk up and listen—and that is what makes it valuable campaign rhetoric.

Forceful campaign rhetoric also spurs people to engage in political debate. The other candidate might run an ad rebutting the charge. Independent groups, including those dreaded super PACs, weigh in. News reporters run fact-checking segments; bloggers and journalists have their say, too. Political ads get people talking and writing to either rebut or confirm the accusations.

This is how it should be. A guiding First Amendment principle is that the proper response to "bad" speech is more speech.

Allowing the government to regulate misleading, inaccurate or negative speech not only puts too much trust in government officials who have a vested interested in curtailing speech directed against them, it puts too little trust in the American people.

4

Corporations Aren't Persons

Matthew Rothschild

Matthew Rothschild, editor of The Progressive, *a peace and social justice magazine, has appeared on* Nightline, The O'Reilly Factor, *and National Public Radio. Rothschild hosts* Progressive Radio *and* Progressive Point of View, *nationally syndicated radio talk shows, and is author of* You Have No Rights: Stories of America in an Age of Repression.

Corporations are not people and thus have no right to free speech in the form of campaign contributions to super political action committees (PACs). Nevertheless, in the Citizens United *decision, despite the intent of the nation's founders to prevent corporations from corrupting the democratic process, the Supreme Court concluded that corporations are entitled to free speech and pose no threat to the political system. The Court's reasoning is flawed and without precedent. Giving corporations with large treasuries the power to influence electoral politics through super PACs undermines the concept of a representative government. Democracy cannot survive if corporations unduly influence the government to promote their own interests at the expense of the people. Because the Supreme Court is unlikely to overturn its decision, and the decision is now the law of the land, the only way to prevent corporations from using their vast resources to drown out the voices of American voters is to amend the Constitution.*

On February 16, [2010] about 200 people gathered on the steps of the Wisconsin state capitol. "It's fitting that we stand out in the cold," said Mike McCabe, executive director of the Wisconsin Democracy Campaign. "That's where the Supreme Court has left us."

He was referring to the court's recent decision in *Citizens United v. Federal Election Commission*, which granted corporations the right to spend unlimited funds on so-called independent expenditures to influence the outcome of elections. The crowd heartily agreed with McCabe. Signs said: "No Corporate Takeover of Elections," "Free Speech, Not Fee Speech," "Money Is Not Speech, Corporations Are Not Persons." And a chant went up: "Overrule the Court."

Corporations do not have the same rights as persons.

Ben Manski, executive director of the Liberty Tree Foundation, drew the crowd in with a historical analogy.

"Susan B. Anthony, the great suffragist and abolitionist, was born" on February 15, 1820, he said. "Were she alive now, she would be here, celebrating with us, marching to overrule the Court. On a future day, a multitude will gather on these same steps and look back at what we here dare to do, and they will thank you."

What the crowd was daring to do was nothing less than kick off a nationwide grassroots campaign to amend the Constitution not only to overturn the court's reckless decision but also to state, once and for all, that corporations do not have the same rights as persons.

Make no mistake about it: The court's ruling in *Citizens United*, if left to stand, will destroy whatever hope we may ever have had of democracy in this country. It will entrench corporate power as never before. And the promise of America will be dashed.

Fighting Bob La Follette, the great Senator from Wisconsin and the founder of this magazine, warned throughout his career about the looming threat posed by corporate power. When he ran for President in 1924, he said: "Democracy cannot live side by side with the control of government by private monopoly. We must choose, on the one hand, between representative government, with its guarantee of peace, liberty, and economic freedom and prosperity for all the people, and on the other, war, tyranny, and the impoverishment of the many for the enrichment of the favored few."

Yes, we must choose.

And we must choose now.

To read the 5–4 majority decision in *Citizens United* is to look at a fun-house mirror. The case, most narrowly, concerned whether the rightwing nonprofit group Citizens United, which is partially funded by corporations, could run an anti-Hillary Clinton documentary on cable and whether it could promote the film with ads on TV close to election time. The McCain-Feingold law prohibited corporate-funded independent ads during such a timeframe, and *Citizens United* challenged the constitutionality of the law as it applied to this particular instance.

But the Court's majority was not interested in ruling narrowly. Justice Anthony Kennedy, writing for the majority, threw out decades of Supreme Court precedents. Writing in the most sweeping way, he declared that "political speech of corporations or other associations" cannot "be treated differently under the First Amendment simply because such associations are not 'natural persons.'"

The logic of the Court's argument would throw out all restrictions on corporate expenditures. "Political speech must prevail against laws that would suppress it, whether by design or inadvertence," it said. This seems to justify unlimited direct gifts to candidates, though the majority didn't quite go there. But it went everywhere else.

The decision asserted, astonishingly and without evidence, that "independent expenditures, including those made by corporations, do not give rise to corruption or the appearance of corruption." It added: "The appearance of influence or access, furthermore, will not cause the electorate to lose faith in our democracy." And it asserted that "no sufficient governmental interest justifies limits on the political speech of nonprofit or for-profit corporations."

Although they make enormous contributions to our society, corporations are not actually members of it. They cannot vote or run for office.

Justice John Paul Stevens, at eighty-nine writing eloquently in dissent, warned: "Starting today, corporations with large war chests to deploy on electioneering may find democratically elected bodies becoming much more attuned to their interests." The Court's decision, he added, undermines the integrity of our democratic institutions and "will undoubtedly cripple the ability of ordinary citizens, Congress, and the states to adopt even limited measures to protect against corporate domination of the electoral process."

Stevens cut to the heart of the matter and laid out why corporations should not be treated as persons. "In the context of election to public office, the distinction between corporate and human speakers is significant," he argued. "Although they make enormous contributions to our society, corporations are not actually members of it. They cannot vote or run for office. Because they may be managed and controlled by nonresidents, their interests may conflict in fundamental respects with the interests of eligible voters. . . . Our lawmakers have a compelling constitutional basis, if not also a democratic duty, to take measures designed to guard against the potentially deleterious effects of corporate spending in local and national races." Later, he added, witheringly: "Under the majority's view, I suppose it may be a First Amendment problem that corporations are not permitted to vote, given that voting is, among other things, a form of speech."

Stevens also invoked our Founders. "Unlike our colleagues, they had little trouble distinguishing corporations from human beings, and when they constitutionalized the right to free speech in the First Amendment, it was the free speech of individual Americans that they had in mind," he wrote. "Thomas Jefferson famously fretted that corporations would subvert the Republic," Stevens observed, and in a footnote, he provided the quotation from Jefferson from 1816: "I hope we shall . . . crush in [its] birth the aristocracy of our monied corporations."

By an overwhelming margin, the American people have sided with Justice Stevens and against the Court's majority. According to a *Washington Post*-ABC News poll, 80 percent of the American people oppose the Court's decision, and 65 percent "strongly" oppose it. "The poll shows remarkably strong agreement about the ruling across all demographic groups," noted Dan Eggen of the *Post*. "The poll reveals relatively little difference of opinion on the issue among Democrats (85 percent opposed to the ruling), Republicans (76 percent), and independents (81 percent)."

This represents a huge base of support for overturning the decision.

But how to do it?

Some members of Congress are hoping to blunt the effect of the decision legislatively. Senator Sherrod Brown of Ohio introduced a bill that would require corporations to get prior approval of their shareholders before launching political ads. And Senator Charles Schumer of New York and Representative Chris Van Hollen of Maryland began circulating drafts of legislation that would ban independent campaign expenditures by corporations that are more than 20 percent foreign owned. They would also ban such expenditures by any company that receives taxpayer support through either the Troubled Asset Relief Program or through federal contracts. And their bills would require a great deal more disclosure.

"If we don't act quickly, the Court's ruling will have an immediate and disastrous impact on the 2010 elections," Schumer said. "Our goal is to advance the legislation quickly, otherwise the Supreme Court will have predetermined winners of next November's election—it won't be Republicans, it won't be Democrats, it will be corporate America."

But the Democrats in Congress aren't acting quickly on this. And even if they did, they'd run into an unmovable object: The Supreme Court's decision is now the law of the land. The Court would likely strike down any legislation that went against it.

We must exclude all commercial corporations and other artificial commercial entities from participating in political activities. Such constitutional rights should be reserved for real people.

"These are noble efforts on the Hill, but they misdiagnose the problem," says Lisa Graves, executive director of the Center for Media and Democracy. "We shouldn't waste energy on legislation that won't pass a filibuster or won't pass muster with this five-member majority on the court." (Graves, by the way, calls *Citizens United* "*Bush v. Gore*"[1] on steroids. That decision affected only one, or at most two, elections. This will affect many elections to come.")

1. *Bush v. Gore* is a controversial Supreme Court decision that effectively resolved the dispute surrounding the 2000 presidential election, which allowed Florida's certification of George W. Bush as the winner of Florida's 25 electoral votes thus defeating Al Gore by one more than the required 270 electoral votes. Some claim that only conservative Republican Justices ruled against Gore in this case and did so for partisan reasons. Other analysts note that black-majority precincts had three times as many rejected ballots as white precincts and thus the recount was necessary to ensure equal protection.

There's another approach, floated by [political activist] Ralph Nader and by Robert Weissman, the new president of [citizen advocacy group] Public Citizen. While they support legislative efforts, they say the President could issue an executive order refusing to "contract with or provide subsidies, handouts, and bailouts to any company that spends money directly in the electoral arena."

But the Supreme Court could invalidate such an order, as well.

Nader and Weissman also recommend that shareholders pass resolutions requiring their corporations to receive majority permission before spending money on elections.

Imagine a world where corporations could spend the never-ending source of their corporations' treasuries on elections and campaigns and public policy. The people would completely lose our voice.

Ultimately, however, Nader and Weissman favor amending the Constitution. "In the absence of a future court overturning *Citizens United*," they wrote in *The Wall Street Journal* on February 10, [2010] "the fundamental response should be a constitutional amendment. We must exclude all commercial corporations and other artificial commercial entities from participating in political activities. Such constitutional rights should be reserved for real people."

On February 2, [2010,] Representative Donna Edwards, Democrat of Maryland, became the first member of Congress to offer up a constitutional amendment aimed at *Citizens United*. She introduced the following: "The sovereign right of the people to govern being essential to a free democracy, Congress and the States may regulate the expenditure of funds for political speech by any corporation, limited liability company, or other corporate entity." It was co-sponsored by Representatives André Carson, John Conyers, Keith Ellison, Raúl Grijalva,

Jesse Jackson Jr., Barbara Lee, Ed Markey, Jim McGovern, Eleanor Holmes Norton, Chellie Pingree, and Betty Sutton.

We need to "take matters into our own hands to enact a constitutional amendment that once and for all declares that we the people govern our elections and our campaigns, not we the corporations," Edwards said, in a great video on the website freespeechforpeople.org. "Imagine a world where corporations could spend the never-ending source of their corporations' treasuries on elections and campaigns and public policy. The people would completely lose our voice.... It would be gone."

To illustrate Edwards's point, Jamie Raskin, a Maryland state senator and a law professor at American University, provided the following example on that same video. "In 2008, the Fortune 100 corporations had $600 billion in profits," Raskin said. "Now imagine that those top 100 companies decided to spend a modest 1 percent of their profits to intervene in our politics and to get their way. That would mean $6 billion, or double what the Obama campaign spent, the McCain campaign spent, and every candidate for House and Senate."

On February 24, [2010,] Senator Chris Dodd of Connecticut introduced his own constitutional amendment, which was co-sponsored by Senator Tom Udall of New Mexico. The amendment would "authorize Congress to regulate the raising and spending of money for federal political campaigns, including independent expenditures, and allow states to regulate such spending at their level," according to a statement from Dodd's office.

"Ultimately, we must cut through the underbrush and go directly to the heart of the problem," said Dodd. "And that is why I am proposing this constitutional amendment: because constitutional questions need constitutional answers. I believe it is the best way to save our democratic system of government from the continued corrosion of special interest influence."

Two progressive coalitions are pushing the effort to amend the Constitution. One is at freespeechforpeople.org. According to the website, "this is a campaign sponsored by Voter Action (voteraction.org), Public Citizen (citizen.org), the Center for Corporate Policy (corporatepolicy.org), and American Independent Business Alliance (amiba.net) to restore the First Amendment's free speech guarantees for the people, and to preserve and promote democracy and self-government. We are joined by a growing wave of people around the country."

The other is movetoamend.org. (Disclosure: I signed its petition.) It's a little broader in scope than just overturning *Citizens United*. Here's how it spells out its goals: "We, the People of the United States of America, reject the U.S. Supreme Court's ruling in *Citizens United*, and move to amend our Constitution to:

"Firmly establish that money is not speech, and that human beings, not corporations, are persons entitled to constitutional rights.

"Guarantee the right to vote and to participate, and to have our votes and participation count.

"Protect local communities, their economies, and democracies against illegitimate 'preemption' actions by global, national, and state governments."

Some of the prime movers behind it are the Liberty Tree Foundation, the Center for Media and Democracy, and the Independent Progressive Politics Network. And it is endorsed by the National Lawyers Guild, Progressive Democrats of America, Women's International League for Peace and Freedom, and the Program on Corporations, Law, and Democracy.

There are two ways to amend the Constitution. One is to start with Congress, pass the amendment by a two-thirds margin in both houses, and then get three-quarters of the states to ratify it. The other way, which has almost never been used, is to get two-thirds of the states to call a constitutional convention, and then get three-quarters to ratify.

The Free Speech for People group favors the traditional way, while some in the Move to Amend coalition lean more toward a constitutional convention.

"I certainly think it would be more effective to build up from the states," says Manski. "It may be that in the process of winning state legislatures over, we'll change the political climate and Congress will respond by taking action. But I'm not going to rely on Congress. For myself, the safest route is to put all of our energy into the state initiatives and go the constitutional convention route."

John Bonifaz, the legal director of Voter Action, believes it would be "dangerous to go down that road." A constitutional convention, he fears, could be a disaster for minority rights. He believes that the right wing might successfully organize to pass an amendment declaring marriage as solely between a man and a woman or anointing English as the official language of the United States.

Now is the time for us to put in notion a great popular movement to defend democracy against the champions of corporate plutocracy.

"What we're about is reclaiming our democracy and advancing the franchise, not moving backwards," he says.

The groups are getting along, fortunately, and working together. And they sense the urgency of the moment.

"The Supreme Court has had its say," Raskin said. "Now it's our turn. Now is the time for us to put in motion a great popular movement to defend democracy against the champions of corporate plutocracy."

But no one has any illusions that it will be easy, as anyone who experienced the heartbreak of the Equal Rights Amendment can attest.

"It's certainly an uphill fight," says Weissman. The court's decision "dealt a severe body blow to our democracy, and we'll have to wait and see whether democracy can rise up or falls to the canvas."

Senator Russ Feingold of Wisconsin calls the ruling "one of the most lawless in the history of the Supreme Court." But ever idiosyncratic, Feingold opposes a constitutional amendment as a remedy. "I think that's unwise, but I certainly understand the sentiment," he told *The Progressive*. "The best thing to do is to get new justices, different justices, who will do the right thing."

That may be a shortcut—and it may not.

"Based on the age of some of the justices in the majority, that's suggesting we wait a very long time," says Bonifaz, who has litigated the campaign finance issue at the Supreme Court. "And while a constitutional amendment can take a long time, there have been instances where it took only a few years."

There's one other drawback to hoping for a more enlightened composition of justices, because that leaves the question of corporate personhood up for grabs every time there is a new formation on the Supreme Court.

We need to slay the dragon of corporate personhood once and for all.

To do that, it seems to me, we'll have to put our Susan B. Anthony hats on and get to work.

5

Corporations That Donate Money Have the Right to Political Speech

Jan Witold Baran

Jan Witold Baran, a campaign and election lawyer, is author of
The Election Law Primer for Corporations.

Corporations and unions are entitled to political speech. The Supreme Court decided correctly in Citizens United *that super political action committees (PACs) may engage in unlimited political spending independent of campaigns. This decision increases speech, not corruption. Corporations still cannot give money directly to candidates, and super PAC expenditures must be independent of the candidate's own campaign. However, rather than be limited to ads that ask people to support a candidate's stand on an issue, super PACs can run ads that contain express words to promote a candidate. The decision ends efforts to muzzle speech and discourage the political participation of those who have an interest in the work of elected officials.*

In just seven years, the Supreme Court has declared most of the fabled McCain-Feingold law [which regulates political campaign funding] unconstitutional. The court has struck down the law's bans on contributions by minors, on independent spending by political parties and on issue ads within 30 days of a primary or 60 days of a general election, as well as restrictions on "millionaire" candidates. With last week's [January 21, 2010] ruling in *Citizens United v. Federal Election Commission*, the court has now declared that corporations and unions may spend money on political advertising that urges the election or defeat of a candidate for public office.

The reaction was swift and intense. Conservatives and libertarians praised the ruling's preservation of the First Amendment and freedom of speech. Liberals and reformers expressed horror. President [Barack] Obama predicted a "stampede of special-interest money in our politics" and declared, "I can't think of anything more devastating to the public interest." (Disclosure: I filed a brief with the Supreme Court in support of *Citizens United*.)

Answering the Critics

One would think from all this that corporations and unions are now free to buy candidates on the open market. But what, if anything, will be different in our elections?

Will corporations and unions be able to give money to candidates or political parties? No. Federal law, which regulates campaigns for president, the Senate and the House, prohibits such contributions. The ban was left untouched by the Supreme Court.

Can corporations spend money in cahoots with candidates and political parties? No. The Supreme Court decision addressed only "independent expenditures," which are, by definition, "not coordinated with a candidate." Monies spent in collaboration with candidates or parties are treated as contributions—and are still banned.

Perhaps all of this corporate spending will be secret? Wrong again. The Supreme Court upheld the laws that require any corporate or union spender to file reports with the Federal Election Commission [F.E.C.] within 24 hours of spending the first dime.

What about the "stampede of special-interest money"? The president's comment implies there must not have been any corporate or union spending before *Citizens United*. In fact, in the final days of the Massachusetts special election for senator, corporations and unions spent at least $2.7 million on television and radio advertising. How do we know? Those reports were filed with the F.E.C. And while this was a good deal of spending, it was not unusual.

Corporations and unions can run independent ads that contain words of express advocacy.

The Actual Impact of *Citizens United*

So what will actually occur as a result of the *Citizens United* case? The answer is at once mundane and momentous.

Since the 1970s, Congress has passed an assortment of laws that banned anyone from spending money on independent ads—laws that were uniformly declared unconstitutional when they restricted spending by individuals, political action committees and political parties. But in a 1990 decision, *Austin v. Michigan Chamber of Commerce*, the court upheld a ban on corporate spending to expressly advocate the election or defeat of a candidate.

Because of the 1990 ruling, corporations and unions have been limited to so-called issue ads, which usually end with statements like "call Candidate Jones and tell her"—take your choice—"to stop raising taxes/support health care reform/ support alternative energy sources." Now that *Citizens United* has overturned *Austin*, corporations and unions can run independent ads that contain words of express advocacy. So instead of "Call Candidate Jones and demand that she not raise taxes," it can be: "Vote for Candidate Smith because Candidate Jones wants to raise taxes."

There is also no factual basis to predict that there will be a "stampede" of additional spending. As the court noted, 26 states and the District of Columbia already permit independent corporate and union campaign spending. There have been no stampedes in those states' elections. Having a constitutional right is not the same as requiring one to exercise it, and there are many reasons businesses and unions may not spend much more on politics than they already do. As such, the effect of *Citizens United* on the 2010 campaigns is debatable.

The greatest benefit of Citizens United *is that it will restrain Congress from flooding us with arcane, burdensome, convoluted campaign laws that discourage political participation.*

A Message to Congress

However, the effect of *Citizens United* on further legislative meddling with campaign speech is clear. In recent years, Congress interpreted its power to regulate campaigns as a license to limit, restrict, burden and confuse anyone who wished to engage in political campaigns.

But the court has reminded us that the First Amendment is not a license to regulate—it is a limitation on Congress. As the court said in its ruling, "The First Amendment does not permit laws that force speakers to retain a campaign finance attorney, conduct demographic marketing research, or seek declaratory rulings before discussing the most salient political issues of our day."

While this may be disheartening to Washington lawyers and lawmakers, it should be a breath of fresh air to everyone else. The greatest benefit of *Citizens United* is that it will restrain Congress from flooding us with arcane, burdensome, convoluted campaign laws that discourage political participation.

The history of campaign finance reform is the history of incumbent politicians seeking to muzzle speakers, any speakers, particularly those who might publicly criticize them and their legislation. It is a lot easier to legislate against unions, gun owners, "fat cat" bankers, health insurance companies and any other industry or "special interest" group when they can't talk back.

6

Speech of Super PAC Donors Drowns Out the Speech of Average Americans

Blair Bowie and Adam Lioz

Blair Bowie is an advocate with US PIRG, a consumer group whose goal is to counter threats posed by powerful interests. Adam Lioz is an attorney and campaign finance advocate with Demos, a public policy organization that promotes political and economic equality.

Super political action committees (PACs) threaten the democratic principle of political equality. Through super PACs, corporations, unions and other groups may engage in unlimited political spending independent of campaigns. In fact, in the 2012 election, super PACs outspent small donors so significantly that their political voices reached 23,000 times the volume of the average small donor. Moreover, tracing the source of this money is difficult, making it challenging for voters to judge the credibility of super PAC political messages. Super PAC campaign spending increases the political influence of the wealthy few. Polls show that Americans believe corporations have too much political influence, threatening the principle of 'one person, one vote.'

A small wealthy elite has long dominated campaign funding, but Super PACs [political action committees] have made a bad situation much worse. Now, a billionaire who wishes to help a friend, associate, or ideological ally get elected to federal office can contribute an unlimited amount to a Super PAC closely aligned (although not technically coordinated) with her favorite candidate's campaign. In addition the "merely rich" can make their voices heard loud and clear by contributing $20,000 or $50,000 for a single election—drowning out the voices of average citizens and ensuring that the candidate or candidates they support have a better chance to win. And, candidates know they need to court these wealthy donors in order to remain competitive, enabling this "donor class" to shape candidates' agendas and play a critical filtering role.

Large Donor Dominance

In 2012, 58.9% of Super PAC funding came from just 159 donors contributing at least $1 million. More than 93% of the money Super PACs raised came in contributions of at least $10,000—from just 3,318 donors, or the equivalent of 0.0011% of the U.S. population.

A select group of individual millionaires and billionaires has used Super PACs to exert massive influence over federal elections.

In a country of more than 300 million people, nearly all of the money raised by Super PACs came from just a few thousand—less than half the number of people who work at Google's headquarters in Mountain View, California.

In fact, Super PACs provided such a convenient avenue for large donors to dominate the political process that the top 32 Super PAC donors, giving an average of $9.9 million each, matched the $313.0 million that President [Barack] Obama and [Republican presidential nominee] Mitt Romney raised from all of their small donors combined—that's at least 3.7 million people giving less than $200.

In addition, a select group of individual millionaires and billionaires has used Super PACs to exert massive influence over federal elections. For example, 99 people contributed at least $1 million, accounting for nearly 60% of all the individual contributions to Super PACs. . . .

The vast majority of Americans agree that it is critical that we all come to the political table as equals and have an approximately equal say over the decisions that affect our lives.

The Role of Money in a Capitalist Democracy

We live in a representative democracy with a capitalist economy. This means that we hold different values dear in the economic and political spheres.

In the economic sphere, most Americans will tolerate some inequality (and many will tolerate quite a bit), so long as it results from meritocratic competition, because we respect that other values such as efficiency and proper incentives have a role to play in structuring our economy. One's political ideology to a certain extent determines how much inequality one is willing to sanction in the name of other values—with self-identified conservatives generally comfortable with a wider income gap than self-identified liberals or progressives. Few argue that everyone should receive the same income regardless of effort, talent, or other factors.

In the political sphere, on the other hand, equality is a core American value. Regardless of partisan or ideological affiliation, the vast majority of Americans agree that it is critical that we all come to the political table as equals and have an approximately equal say over the decisions that affect our lives. Through multiple amendments and Supreme Court decisions, the concept of political equality ("one person, one vote") has become a core constitutional principle.

But, we cannot maintain a democracy of equal citizens in the face of significant (and rising) economic inequality if we allow those who are successful, or even just lucky, in the economic sphere to translate wealth directly into political power. Our democratic public sphere is where we set the terms for economic competition. It is where we decide—as equals—how much inequality, redistribution, regulation, pollution we will tolerate. These choices gain legitimacy from the fact that we all had the opportunity to have our say. Allowing the already-powerful to rig the rules in favor of their own success undermines the legitimacy of the economic relations in society.

In short, democracy must write the rules for capitalism, not the other way around. And, the only way to ensure this happens is to have some mechanism for preventing wealthy individuals and institutions from translating their wealth into political power. Common sense restrictions on the unfettered use of private wealth for public influence are the bulwarks or firewalls that enable us to maintain our democratic values and a capitalist economy simultaneously. Without these protections, we risk creating a society in which private wealth and public power are one and the same—which looks more like plutocracy than democracy.

Large Donors Use Political Contributions to Dominate Public Policy

Unfortunately we currently lack the key protections we need to prevent private wealth from becoming public power. Through our current campaign finance system, wealthy individuals and special interests are able to translate their policy preferences—which differ from average citizens—into public policy.

The Donor Class Holds Different Policy Preferences

We have long known that large campaign contributors are different than average Americans in important ways. First, they are more likely to be wealthy, white, and male. According to a nationwide survey funded by the Joyce Foundation during the 1996 congressional elections, 81% of those who gave contributions of at least $200 reported annual family incomes greater than $100,000. This stood in stark contrast to the general population at the time, where only 4.6% declared an income of more than $100,000 on their tax returns. Ninety-five percent of contributors surveyed were white and 80% were men.

A growing body of research shows that wealthy Americans have different opinions and priorities than the rest of the nation.

Recent Sunlight Foundation research confirms that ultra-elite donors who give $10,000 or more—"The One Percent of the One Percent"—are quite different than their fellow citizens. In the 2010 election cycle, these 26,783 individuals were responsible for nearly a quarter of all funds contributed to politicians, parties, PACs, and independent expenditure groups. Nearly 55% of these donors were affiliated with corporations and nearly 16% were lawyers or lobbyists. More than 32% of them lived in New York City, Los Angeles, Chicago, San Francisco, or Washington, DC.

And now a growing body of research shows that wealthy Americans have different opinions and priorities than the rest of the nation. Investigators for the Joyce study cited above found that large donors are significantly more conservative than the general public on economic matters, tending to favor tax cuts over anti-poverty spending.

A recent report by the Russell Sage Foundation confirms this finding. The authors surveyed "a small but representative sample of wealthy Chicago-area households." They found meaningful distinctions between the wealthy respondents they surveyed and the general public on key economic issues.

Perhaps the most significant discrepancy between the policy preferences of the wealthy and other Americans is the relative priority each puts on reducing deficits and creating jobs.

For example, wealthy respondents "often tend to think in terms of 'getting government out of the way' and relying on free markets or private philanthropy to produce good outcomes." In spite of majority public support for raising taxes on millionaires, among respondents, "[t]here was little sentiment for substantial tax increases on the wealthy or anyone else." And, in spite of recent scandals on Wall Street, "more than two thirds of [survey] respondents said that the federal government 'has gone too far' in regulating business and the free enterprise system."

A follow up report finds even more evidence of divided preferences on economic issues. For example, more than twice the percentage of the general public than the wealthy believe that "the government should provide a decent standard of living for the unemployed;" and more than three times the percentage of the general public than the wealthy believe that "the government in Washington ought to see to it that everyone who wants to work can find a job."

Given the current conversation in Washington, perhaps the most significant discrepancy between the policy preferences of the wealthy and other Americans is the relative priority each puts on reducing deficits and creating jobs. Significantly more wealthy respondents than average Americans listed deficits as the most important problem facing our country. Among those who did, "none at all referred only to raising revenue. Two thirds (65%) mentioned only cutting spending."

The Wealthy Wield
Disproportionate Influence

It is not surprising that the wealthy have different policy priorities—after all, top-earners do not live or work like most other citizens. It's also unsurprising that these elites have more influence over public policy than average-earning citizens—as they likely do in many aspects of life, probably since the beginning of private wealth. But, a growing body of relatively new research has shown how shockingly disproportionate this influence truly is.

The preferences of people in the bottom third of the income distribution have no apparent impact on the behavior of their elected officials.

In an important new book called *Affluence and Influence*, Princeton political scientist Martin Gilens explores what he terms the "preference/policy link," and examines the varying degree of political influence of Americans at different points on the economic spectrum. Studying decades of public opinion surveys and measuring them against actual policy outcomes, Professor Gilens concludes that "[t]he American government does respond to the public's preferences, but that responsiveness is strongly tilted toward the most affluent citizens." In considering whether this could be because higher-income Americans are more educated and hence more informed on issues, Gilens notes that "[c]learly both income and education matter in determining the strength of the preference/policy link. But equally clearly, income is the more important determinant of how strong the link is."

The flip side to the disproportionate influence of the wealthy is the truly disturbing political impotence of the rest of American society. Gilens writes that "under most circumstances, the preferences of the vast majority of Americans appear to have essentially no impact on which policies the government does or doesn't adopt." "The complete lack of government responsiveness to the preferences of the poor," he notes, "is disturbing and seems consistent only with the most cynical views of American politics." But, this is not just about the powerlessness of the poor. Gilens points out that "median-income Americans fare no better than the poor when their policy preferences diverge from those of the well-off."

Further, just as wealthy individuals' policy preferences diverge most sharply from other Americans around economic issues, this is where their differential influence is at its peak. Gilens finds that "the starkest difference in responsiveness to the affluent and the middle class occurs on economic policy, a consequence of high-income Americans' stronger opposition to taxes and corporate regulation."

Helping to elect likeminded candidates is the most basic way that citizens of all types attempt to influence policy.

Gilens findings are hardly idiosyncratic. In a 2008 book called *Unequal Democracy,* economist Larry Bartels found that "the preferences of people in the bottom third of the income distribution have no apparent impact on the behavior of their elected officials." These studies confirm through rigorous empirical research what many Americans perceive intuitively: a narrow wealthy elite drives political decision-making in America, and most of the rest of us are left on the sidelines.

How Large Donations Translate to Policy Influence

So, the wealthy have more influence. Why? After studying the issue, Gilens concludes that our system of funding elections is a significant source of this inequality of influence, noting that "political donations, but not voting or volunteering, resembles the pattern of representational inequality" that his book has identified and that "any effort to strengthen the influence of less-affluent Americans over federal policy must address the highly skewed sources of individual campaign donations."

There are two primary ways that large donors are able to wield influence. First, donors help candidates who share their views win election, and hence assume positions of power. Helping to elect likeminded candidates is the most basic way that citizens of all types attempt to influence policy. This is the motivation for the vast majority of the millions of Americans who make political contributions, large and small, each election cycle. Making donations for this reason is similar to exercising one's right to vote—except of course that while every eligible citizen can in theory exert an equal political voice through the franchise, not everyone has an equal ability to contribute money.

Money does not guarantee victory, but all else equal, it improves a candidate's prospects. It is nearly impossible for a candidate to run a competitive race without raising a threshold amount of money. And, although there are diminishing returns, more is likely better. If nothing else, the constant fundraising arms races shows that those with the most at stake in the game—candidates and their staff and political consultants—believe money to be a key factor critical to success. And, as long as key players believe money to be important, it is—if for no other reason than that this belief shapes their behavior.

7

Super PACs May Further Constrain a Polarized Congress

Dan Glickman

Dan Glickman, a businessman and politician, is currently a fellow at the Bipartisan Policy Center and co-chair of the center's democracy project. He was chairman and chief executive officer of the Motion Picture Association of America (MPAA) from 2004 to 2010, served as the US Secretary of Agriculture from 1995 to 2001, and represented Kansas in Congress for eighteen years.

The failure of Congress to make decisions on issues of concern to many Americans has made the body unpopular. Super political action committees (PACs), corporations, unions, and other groups that may engage in unlimited political spending independent of campaigns, may further inhibit Congress by using these unlimited funds to defeat a candidate who votes favorably on an issue the group opposes. Super PACs may aim to control the political process by making it difficult for members of Congress to vote on controversial positions or be willing to compromise, further constraining Congress. In order to tackle the problems facing our nation, members of Congress need to be able to lead and make difficult decisions without worrying about the size of the check a super PAC is willing to write to oppose them.

Much has been made of the impact that Super PACs [political action committees] are having on the 2012 presidential race, not least of all by me. We already know that Super PACs can enable extraordinarily wealthy donors to keep longshot presidential candidacies alive by providing enormous checks used to blanket states with predominantly negative advertising. Realistically, the impact is likely to be far greater on Congress.

Enter the Super PACs

Congress isn't the most beloved institution these days, with popularity ratings hovering between root canals and Fidel Castro.[1] Congress is somewhat deserving of this low rating for a lot of reasons, but in large part because of its inability to pass budgets, raise the debt ceiling or confirm presidential nominees. Enter Super PACs.

Incumbents may have a more difficult time maintaining their seats thanks to Super PACs. Just ask Reps. Jean Schmidt (R), Spencer Bachus (R) or Jesse Jackson Jr. (D), each of whom faced primary opponents that received funding from the Super PAC called the "Campaign for Primary Accountability." This particular Super PAC spent $250,000 to oust Rep. Bachus, but he survived. Rep. Schmidt, on the other hand, ended up losing her primary to Brad Wenstrup, an Iraq war veteran and political novice. If Mr. Wenstrup ends up winning the general election, should he expect the Campaign for Primary Accountability to send thousands of dollars to *his* primary opponent in 2014? [He won.]

It's not clear, but what is clear is that Super PACs do have the power to intervene in congressional races, where Super PAC dollars can make an even bigger splash than in the na-

1. Fidel Castro, a communist revolutionary and politician, was prime minister of Cuba from 1959 to 1976, and president from 1976 to 2008. Under his administration the Republic of Cuba became a one-party socialist state. Castro has been heavily criticized, particularly in the Western world.

tional Presidential race. Maybe this is a good way to create genuine competition in congressional races which have historically been non-competitive. But more likely it will be a way for a few very wealthy contributors to increasingly control the political process.

One consequence of Super PACs entering the congressional campaign arena will be that Congress becomes more constrained than it is even now.

A Potentially Crippling Impact

If Super PACs can successfully intervene in Congressional races, and have an even greater impact on them because of their smaller regional scope, it's not a stretch of the imagination to forsee Members of Congress having hundreds of thousands of Super PAC dollars thrown against them as the result of a single vote on a controversial issue. More significantly, big corporations, industry groups, labor unions, wealthy individuals or organizations could easily create Super PACs that promise to lend their substantial financial weight to any opponent of a Member of Congress who votes to eliminate a tax subsidy, a spending item, or a vote on a social issue that a group or individual favors. Imagine how crippling it would be if Members of Congress become increasingly fixated each week of their congressional career about the size of the check their opponent's campaign receives by voting a certain way on a certain issue; even months and months before an election.

Being a Congressman today has a lot of challenges I didn't face when I was in the House: increasingly polarized redistricting, the expansion of 24 hour news channels, much stronger party identification and decreasing tolerance for making "independent" decisions, but in my judgment, the influx of huge sums of money is the biggest change. The job is tough enough under the best of circumstances.

Will Super PACs, representing those huge sums of money, paralyze the ability of Members of Congress to even propose a vote for a controversial position? Will it mean that during each two year House term, or six year Senate term, thousands of dollars will continually be dropped into congressional races after every single vote? Will it make Members even more risk averse and unwilling to make compromises? The United States has major obstacles, from our growing debt to our fragile economy and beyond. Congress must be able to function appropriately in order to tackle these problems, and lead when necessary on tough problems such as deficit reduction.

I fear that one consequence of Super PACs entering the congressional campaign arena will be that Congress becomes more constrained than it is even now. In 20 years we will look back and say that the introduction of Super PACs to our political system was a huge mistake. Of course, if I could predict the future I wouldn't be so worried about my NCAA [National Collegiate Athletic Association] tournament bracket.[2] For the sake of our political system and the country, I hope I'm wrong.

2. The author refers to the challenge of predicting among many college basketball teams which team will reach the finals in March.

8

Defending *Citizens United*

Anthony Dick

Anthony Dick is associate editor at National Review, *a conservative news and commentary magazine.*

In Citizens United, *the Supreme Court concluded that the First Amendment prohibits the government from restricting political expenditures by corporations, associations, or labor unions that are independent of political campaigns. Contrary to arguments against the decision, the Court did not engage in judicial activism but exercised its judicial responsibility to ensure that the US Congress respects the US Constitution. First Amendment protection does extend beyond individuals to groups and associations. The wealth of speakers does not limit their right to speak on issues that concern them. In fact, loosening restrictions on corporate speech might encourage companies to pursue their policy objectives more openly rather than operating through less transparent methods such as lobbying. Polls show that most people agree that the government should not protect citizens from hearing messages from powerful interests through restrictions on political spending.*

Bad arguments have been proliferating in the wake of this week's *Citizens United* case, which struck down restrictions on political expenditures by corporations and unions. The opinion leaves in place limits on campaign donations, but frees up corporations and unions to spend as much as they like to disseminate political messages. Here is a rogue's gallery of the most common arguments I've heard against the holding, followed by brief explanations of their profound misguidedness.

1. This 5-4 decision is a blatant example of judicial activism, and conservatives are hypocritical for supporting it. Judicial activism occurs when judges abandon constitutional or statutory meaning and impose their policy preferences instead. A decision that faithfully applies the First Amendment is not activism but rather a proper exercise of the judicial responsibility to keep Congress within its constitutional bounds. The government argued in *Citizens United* that it had the power to outlaw books and movies produced by unions and corporations, both non-profit and for-profit, if they included even a single line addressing an election or a political issue. Such blatant censorship of core political speech falls well within the text and original meaning of the First Amendment, which supported an open marketplace of ideas by declaring in broad terms that "Congress shall make no law . . . abridging the freedom of speech." Contrast this with the paradigmatic examples of left-wing judicial activism, which have manufactured a host of "fundamental" rights without anything resembling such a clear textual basis.

2. Political expenditures are not "speech" and should not be protected under the First Amendment. The force of this seductive argument evaporates upon the realization that spending money is an indispensable component of effective political speech, especially when it involves any audience above a trivial size. If the government could ban expenditures related to speech, it could easily circumvent the First Amendment simply by targeting the necessary funding underlying any communication. Imag-

ine the *New York Times* being prohibited from paying for its writers, production, advertising, and distribution. Wonderful as this might sound in some of its particulars, you can see how the paper's right to free expression might be crimped. And so it goes for any person or group wishing to disseminate a political message through print or broadcast media, which is why the Court has properly subsumed the right to political expenditures within the right to free speech.

3. The protections of the Free Speech Clause properly apply only to individuals, not corporations. [Supreme Court] Justice Scalia dispatched with this argument nicely in his concurring opinion by pointing out that the First Amendment has long been extended beyond isolated individuals to groups and associations whose members gather for a wide variety of purposes ranging from political to commercial. The Democratic party, the Sierra Club, and the *New York Times* aren't individuals, but their speech nonetheless falls under the umbrella of First Amendment protection. But the formalistic obsession with whether a corporation should have the legal status of a "person" with a "right" to free speech quite misses the substantive issues at stake, which concern how the principle of free expression should be applied to the political speech of certain types of social groups. In particular, is there something uniquely harmful and/or unworthy of protection about political messages that come from corporations and unions, as opposed to, say, rich individuals, persuasive writers, or charismatic demagogues? Which brings us to our next point:

4. A deluge of corporate and union speech will corrupt the democratic process. The very idea that political speech in an open democracy can be "corrupting" rests on fundamentally illiberal assumptions about individuals' ca-

pacity for reasoned deliberation and self-government. The First Amendment was designed to allow all speakers to put their messages out into the public debate, be they rich or poor, vicious or virtuous. The underlying principle is that over the long run, a society of free individuals is best equipped to evaluate the merits of political arguments for themselves, and that a distrustful government cannot ban speech out of the worry that its citizens will be unduly swayed by it. Rich individuals and talented polemicists have always been permitted to put out quantities and qualities of speech that may exert a disproportionate influence on society, but political opponents and voters have always been trusted to evaluate these speakers' arguments for themselves, respond with counter-arguments, and ultimately make up their own minds about the truth of any matter of controversy. Especially with the explosion of diverse viewpoints and avenues of expression that have come from the Internet media revolution, it simply defies common sense to think that any corporation or union could ever hope to so overwhelm the political debate as to prevent dissenting voices from being heard and reasonably contemplated by the electorate. Of course, this freewheeling political dialogue may be messy, imperfect, and prone to abuses, but the First Amendment makes it constitutionally preferable to censorship targeted at disfavored groups.

5. This decision will radically increase powerful corporate influence in politics, compared to the status quo. History and economics together suggest that powerful corporate interests operating under an extensive regulatory state will always find a way to exert a strong influence in politics. Up until now, campaign-finance regulations have had two ugly impacts: First, they have imposed huge legal costs on those wishing to participate in the

political process, effectively shutting out smaller voices who cannot afford to pay campaign lawyers and risk legal trouble in getting their messages across. Loosening legal restrictions on smaller businesses will now allow them to enter the marketplace of political ideas on a more equal footing with their larger competitors. Second, campaign-expenditure limits have driven corporate money away from public dialogue and into channels that have been more corrosive and less transparent (think lobbyists, lawsuits, and regulatory capture). While these more pernicious forms of corporate influence are not likely to disappear any time soon, they may be mitigated to the extent that corporations can now pursue their policy objectives through a more open, deliberative process.

6. Corporate political expenditures violate shareholders' rights to withhold funds from messages they disagree with. Two problems here. First, like members of any free association, shareholders have an absolute and easy-to-exercise right to exit from any corporation—in this instance, by simply selling their shares and relocating their investments. It is true that mutual funds and retirement accounts can complicate things, but shareholders maintain the ultimate legal right of control over their assets, including initial investment decisions. In any event, the level of "message subsidy" involved in most of these cases will be so diffuse as to be negligible, especially when compared to government policies and messages that taxpayers must fund despite strong disagreement. Second, corporations commonly disseminate nonpolitical messages and make corporate decisions, including charitable donations, that might strongly offend shareholders. This is tolerated as part of the trade-off inherent in the structure of corporate governance, wherein shareholders voluntarily surrender control of their

companies' day-to-day operations in exchange for the efficiencies of corporate decision-making.

7. This decision will harm Republicans by rallying public opinion in favor of populist-progressive reform and against the "conservative" Supreme Court majority that decided the case. While four members of the *Citizens United* majority might fairly be called conservatives, the actual author of the opinion was Justice Kennedy, who defies easy political categorization. In the past few years, he has been repeatedly toasted in liberal circles for penning such sweeping decisions as *Lawrence v. Texas* and *Kennedy v. Louisiana*, declaring a constitutional right to sodomy and forbidding the death penalty for non-homicidal child rape, respectively. At the very least, those opinions give him some credibility as an independent voice. But perhaps more importantly, a recent Gallup poll shows that a majority of the public actually agrees with the Court that corporations and unions should be treated just like individuals in terms of their political-expenditure rights, and that the government should not attempt to protect its citizens from hearing seductive messages put out by sinister, powerful interests.

9

The *Citizens United* Decision That Supports Super PAC Spending Is Flawed

David Kairys

David Kairys, a law professor at Temple University and a leading civil rights lawyer, is the author of Philadelphia Freedom, Memoir of a Civil Rights Lawyer.

In Citizens United, *the Supreme Court held that corporations, unions, and other groups may engage in unlimited political spending independent of campaigns. The Court based its decision on two flawed theories—money is speech and corporations are people. Money is not speech but a rhetorical device that gives First Amendment protection to the wealthy. By increasing the speech rights of the wealthy, the Court restricts the speech of people of ordinary means. The idea that corporations are people also is incorrect, as the political spending of corporate executives does not necessarily reflect the views of shareholders. These theories are not about constitutional rights but invalidating campaign finance reforms to increase the political power of wealthy corporate leaders.*

Go back almost a century, to the time when the modern corporation was created, and you'll find laws that prohibit or limit the use of corporate money in elections. And yet this week, a 5–4 Supreme Court struck down the limits that Congress passed in 2002 in this tradition in the case *Citizens United v. FEC* [Federal Election Commission].

Strange, Wrongheaded Theories

The majority's ruling unleashes a new wave of campaign cash and adds to the already considerable power of corporations. The court's main rationale is that limits on using corporate treasuries for campaigns are a "classic example of censorship," as Justice Anthony Kennedy wrote for the majority. To get there, Kennedy depends on two legal theories that blossomed as constitutional principles in the mid-1970s: money is speech and corporations are people. Both theories are strange, if not simply wrongheaded—why, according to the Constitution or common sense, would money be speech or corporations be people? The court has also employed theories not uniformly but, rather, as constitutional cover for dominance of the electoral system by corporations and by the wealthy.

The money-is-speech theory turns out to be a rhetorical device used exclusively to provide First Amendment protection for all money that wealthy people and businesses want to give to, or to spend, on campaigns.

The first theory appeared in a 1976 decision, *Buckley v. Valeo*, which invalidated some campaign-finance reforms that came out of Watergate.[1] The Court concluded that most limits on campaign expenditures, and some limits on donations, are unconstitutional because money is itself speech and the "quantity of expression"—the amounts of money—can't be limited.

Protecting Wealthy Speech

But in subsequent cases, the conservative justices who had emphatically embraced the money-is-speech principle didn't apply it to money solicited by speakers of ordinary means. For example, the court limited the First Amendment rights of

1. Watergate was a political scandal wherein a break-in occurred at the Democratic National Committee, and the administration of President Richard Nixon attempted to cover up its involvement.

Hare Krishna leafleters soliciting donations in airports to support their own leafleting. The leafleting drew no money-is-speech analysis. To the contrary, the conservative justices, led by Chief Justice [William] Rehnquist, found that by asking for money for leafleting—their form of speech—the Hare Krishnas were being "disruptive" and posing an "inconvenience" to others. In other words, in the court's view' some people's money is speech; others' money is annoying. And the conservative justices have raised no objection to other limits on the quantity of speech, such as limits on the number of picketers.

The money-is-speech theory turns out to be a rhetorical device used exclusively to provide First Amendment protection for all money that wealthy people and businesses want to give to, or to spend, on campaigns. It also doesn't make sense under long established free-speech law. Spending or donating money to support or facilitate speech is expressive and deserves some protection. But money simply doesn't make it into the category of things that are and embody speech, such as books, films, or blogs. Traditional speech-law analysis would separate the speech from the conduct (or "nonspeech") elements of campaign spending and donation and allow considerable leeway to regulate the latter. Even as to "pure" speech, "compelling" government interests are overriding. And spending and donating money seem, among the traditional speech-law categories, a "manner" of speaking that the court has said usually can be "reasonably regulated."

Controversial Innovation

The other basic theory supporting the ruling in *Citizens United*—the court's claim that, for some purposes, corporations are constitutionally, if not actually, people—comes out of the long history of the development of corporations. But the extension of corporate personhood to campaign speech is a controversial innovation of the conservative justices over the last few decades.

Corporations needed some rights usually reserved for people to function as legal entities, so that they could, for instance, make enforceable contracts and sue or be sued. But despite the common cultural personification of corporations—we can easily say "GM [General Motors] was embarrassed today"—they obviously don't and shouldn't have all the rights of people. For example, they don't have the right to vote.

In *Citizens United*, Justice Kennedy discusses business corporations as if they were clubs or political associations with political viewpoints and elected leaders. But corporate managers don't function as representatives or employees or shareholders, who have no say, no shared political views, and no expectation that their investments will be used for political ends. In the wake of the court's ruling this week, will some corporations pick a party or politics while others channel unheard of amounts of money to both major parties? Will investors be influenced by a corporation's political portfolio?

> *This line of cases is about dominance of the political and electoral system by wealthy people and corporations and about legitimizing a political and electoral system that is unrepresentative, money-driven, corrupt, outmoded, and dysfunctional.*

The *Citizens United* decision will make it harder to achieve reforms opposed by major corporations and change business as well as politics. Increasing the constitutional rights of corporations beyond their business purposes is really about increasing the rights and power of corporate managers. Government has enabled corporate managers to control huge accumulations of wealth without any personal risk—an arrangement that contributes to wild, bubble-producing economic swings and collapses. *Citizens United* invites that arrangement directly into politics and elections.

Both of these theories—that money is speech and that corporations are people—have an easier time than they should in courts and with the public, too, because they are posed as counters to censorship. Many of us, including me, haven't seen a free-speech argument we don't like, at least initially.

Looking for Perspective on Free Speech

But some perspective: We limit speech—when it has nothing to do with wealthy people spending money—in many ways. (It wasn't protected at all until the mid-1930s.) You famously can't shout fire in a theater. You not-so-famously can't break the theater's rules, including rules about speaking, because you don't really have any First Amendment rights in a privately owned theater or at work. The First Amendment limits only government. And even where it is fully protected, free speech has not been absolute; it's subject to regulation when it undermines basic societal interests and functions, like voting and democracy. In the last few decades, the conservative justices dominating the court have also limited speech rights for demonstrators, students, and whistle blowers. They have restricted speech at shopping malls and transit terminals. Taken as a whole, the conservative court's First Amendment jurisprudence has enlarged the speech rights available to wealthy people and corporations and restricted the speech rights available to people of ordinary means and to dissenters.

In a largely unnoticed rewriting of speech law, the conservative justices have applied their theories and doctrines inconsistently and selectively, as they have money-is-speech. Some of the conservatives' recent innovations would seem to validate campaign finance laws. The "secondary effects" doctrine, for example, allows government to restrict speech if government can suggest a general, non-speech-related purpose, even if the real purpose is speech-related. The court ignored this doctrine in *Citizens United* and other campaign finance cases—even though campaign finance reform is aimed not at speech itself, but at large amounts of money that skew, corrupt, and undermine elections.

The court's invalidation of campaign finance reforms over the last few decades isn't about censorship or suppressed speakers or viewpoints. At its core, this line of cases is about dominance of the political and electoral system by wealthy people and corporations and about legitimizing a political and electoral system that is unrepresentative, money-driven, corrupt, outmoded, and dysfunctional. Wealthy people and corporate managers shouldn't dominate politics or have more and better speech rights than the rest of us. That seems like an obvious truth. And yet the Supreme Court's recent decisions move us away from it.

10

Failure to Enforce Regulations Makes Super PACs More Powerful

John Avlon, Michael Keller and Daniel Stone

John Avlon is a senior columnist for Newsweek *and the* Daily Beast *and anchor of Beast TV. Michael Keller is senior data reporter at* Newsweek *and the* Daily Beast. *Daniel Stone is a* Newsweek *and* Daily Beast *contributor.*

Super political action committees (PACs) are funded by corporations, unions, and other groups that may engage in unlimited political spending independent of campaigns. The tools needed to restrain super PACs are either ineffectual or not suited to the task. For example, the six members of the Federal Election Commission (FEC)—three Republicans and three Democrats—refuse to compromise on campaign finance decisions. The Internal Revenue Service (IRS) is not likely to audit the spending of tax-exempt organizations that allow for unlimited, anonymous donations and even if it did, the audit would come years after the election. Congress is so constrained that the transparency of super PACs is unlikely to increase. In truth, only a constitutional amendment can counter the deluge of anonymous negative ads. Instead of the hoped for transparency, the political system is steeped in secret money.

The gold rush excesses of the super-PAC [political action committee] economy are encouraged by a Wild West mentality, where all boundaries are pushed in the absence of strong laws. The mechanisms for enforcing the rules are toothless and totally unsuited for the task at hand.

The Federal Election Commission [FEC] would seem to be the obvious agency to regulate the system, but experts say the odds that it will hand down harsh penalties for, say, illegal coordination between a super PAC and a campaign are extremely low. In recent years, the FEC—which is run by six commissioners, three Republicans and three Democrats—has been routinely deadlocked with party-line votes.

"There was always a partisan split on the agency. But there used to be more of an institutional concern that we have a law here to enforce," says Larry Noble, who served as general counsel to the FEC for 13 years. "What happened in the 2000s is that commissioners were appointed who were very upfront about the fact that they didn't believe in the law—and they felt the election laws were unconstitutional in many respects. . . . Over the past ten years or so, you've had a great increase in three/three splits due to the fact that they won't compromise. And so you have a less aggressive commission."

It's not like the IRS could reverse the election results.

If the FEC isn't going to aggressively regulate this world, who will? Another possibility is the IRS [Internal Revenue Service], specifically the tax-exempt division, which oversees the approximately 1.6 million organizations in the United States that claim tax-exempt status—about 97,000 of which are 501(c)(4)s.[1] . . . Some of those C4s—which allow for unlimited, anonymous donations—are playing pivotal roles in the

1. Tax-exempt organizations designated 501(c)(4) are created to promote social welfare. They also may participate in political campaigns, as long as social welfare is their primary activity. They are not required to disclose donors.

2012 campaign. This puts the IRS tax-exempt division in a position to enforce certain rules of the campaign finance system—for instance, the regulation that says C4s can only spend 50 percent of their budget on direct political activity.

The Challenge of Auditing Nonprofits

But is the IRS capable of doing this effectively? The agency's tax-exempt division has about 900 employees—of those, only about 400 to 500 conduct audits. Last year [2011], they conducted about 2,500 audits, but the number of C4 organizations audited is much lower. Depending on the year, the IRS generally audits 100 of the 97,000 C4s annually, meaning there is a roughly 0.1 percent chance that any organization will be audited.

"In any given year, the vast majority of organizations aren't going to hear from the IRS," says Marcus Owens, a Washington lawyer and the former head of the tax-exempt division. "Many organizations will never hear from the IRS over their institutional lives." Normally, the lack of institutional intrusion into a legitimate non-profit would be welcome—but in the case of dark money-spreading 501(c)(4)s, which are pushing the boundaries of the 50-percent rule in order to maximize their impact on elections, there is a need for greater scrutiny.

Even if a C4 *does* get audited, the audit likely won't be completed for nearly two years after the calendar year of the election. And even if the group is found to have broken the law, there are rarely criminal penalties. Instead, there are usually only civil penalties: A C4 group can be stripped of its tax-exempt status and may have to pay back taxes for all of its activities during an election. That might be a lot of money, but for an already wealthy group, that's a small price to pay for a year long offensive to get its favorite candidate elected. And, of course, it's not like the IRS could reverse the election results.

A Lack of Resources

Owens says his former division simply doesn't have the resources to oversee political groups participating in elections. Bill Allison, editorial director of the Sunlight Foundation, puts it this way: "The IRS simply does not want to be in the same business as the FEC."

Top IRS officials declined to answer questions from *The Daily Beast* about the agency's role in election oversight. But a source familiar with IRS internal operations told us that earlier this summer, Lois Lerner, who currently heads the tax-exempt division, held a full staff meeting to discuss the problem on the agency's hands. At the meeting, she said that she and top officials were working on some way to more effectively enforce the law.

In June [2012], after receiving formal complaints about the abuse of 501(c)(4)s co-signed by the liberal organization Democracy 21 and the conservative Campaign Legal Center, the IRS announced that it would send out a questionnaire to "social welfare organizations, labor unions and trade associations" that have attracted unprecedented donations in the past two election cycles in order to collect information about tax compliance and anticipate future audit trends. In July, the IRS issued a letter, publicly affirming its interest in updating these regulations, saying that they "are aware of current public interest in this issue. These regulations have been in place since 1959. We will consider proposed changes in this area."

Besides the IRS, what other avenues are available for bringing some clarity and transparency to the world of campaign finance? One such attempt was a suit brought by Representative Chris Van Hollen (D-MD). That suit resulted in a district court ruling that 501(c)(4)s had to disclose the names of donors whose money paid for electioneering ads within 60 days of a general election and 30 days of a primary election or nominating convention. But this week, that ruling was struck down by a federal appeals court. The FEC has been entrusted with devising new rules—but for now at least, the disclosure requirement is no longer operative.

There are no shortage of other pragmatic proposals to fix the campaign finance system. Trevor Potter, the president of the Campaign Legal Center and former FEC chairman, suggests that Congress take the simple step of requiring C4s to disclose their donors when their money goes toward political advertising. Another proposal—pushed by Senator Maria Cantwell (D-WA)—would apply a gift tax to contributions to 501(c)(4)s. The idea is that the prospect of paying 35 percent on these donations (over a proposed $5 million limit) might dissuade the mega-rich from making outsized, anonymous gifts going forward. For his part, tax-exempt lawyer Gregory Colvin suggests lowering the amount that 501(c)(4)s can spend on politics from 49 percent to 10 percent.

Then there is the DISCLOSE Act [Democracy Is Strengthened by Casting Light on Spending in Elections], which would have required tax-exempt organizations that are involved in political advertising to disclose the names of donors who gave more than $10,000 to that effort. But Senate Republicans blocked the legislation by threatening a filibuster in July [2012]. And, despite rhetoric from [Senator] Mitch McConnell [R-KY] about the importance of transparency in the past, the DISCLOSE Act seems dead in the water going forward.

Post Election Scrutiny

Finally, of course, there is the hope of a more aggressive FEC. Given the FEC's partisan stalemate, it seems unlikely to take strong action in the near future. But it would not be unprecedented. After the 2004 election, action was taken against three 527s—Swiftboat Veterans for Truth, MoveOn.org, and the League of Conservation Voters—on charges that they failed to file disclosure reports as federal political committees and accepted contributions in violation of federal limits.[1] The

---

1. Organizations designated as 527s are tax-exempt groups created primarily to influence elections.

$600,000 levied in penalties was small in comparison to the money spent during the election, but the fines still served as a powerful brush-back pitch to 527s, effectively changing their behavior in the 2006 and 2008 elections.

Instead of seeing a new era of transparency in political donations, our system is awash in both money and secrecy: the worst of both worlds from a citizen's perspective.

This precedent of post-election scrutiny has some lawyers advising clients not to play too fast and loose with the current law. "There are always going to be groups who push the envelope of what's legal on both sides of the partisan divide," says Larry Levy, an election and white-collar defense lawyer in New York. "And that's why I wouldn't be surprised if there are people after this election who find themselves spending a lot of time with the FEC, the IRS, and possibly the DOJ [Department of Justice]—trying to explain what they did and why."

The Supreme Court has spoken on *Citizens United*. Barring a constitutional amendment, it is the law of the land. But the rise of 501(c)(4)s that rarely disclose donors while funding an avalanche of negative ads clearly undercuts the original intention of the ruling. And because of too often toothless regulations, what is not explicitly forbidden is now essentially allowed.

Instead of seeing a new era of transparency in political donations, our system is awash in both money *and* secrecy: the worst of both worlds from a citizen's perspective. This is further polarizing our politics because the super-PAC economy is designed to financially reward hyper-partisanship.

For the consultant class, of course, this is the best of times—as like-minded billionaires and special-interest groups pay them handsomely. But at some point, after this election, the music may well stop. "There will be a test case soon," says

Republican strategist Rick Wilson. "It's why I pay two separate election lawyers to keep me out of jail. Because there will be some eager little bureaucrat who decides that he will end all this horrible negative communication."

11

A Constitutional
Amendment Is Necessary
to Restore Democracy

Bernie Sanders and Robert Weissman

Bernie Sanders is a US Senator from Vermont. Robert Weissman, president of Public Citizen, an organization dedicated to consumer rights, has written extensively about how corporations influence the political process.

A constitutional amendment is necessary to restore democracy and overturn the Citizens United *Supreme Court decision that gave birth to super political action committees (PACs). In* Citizens United, *the Supreme Court skewed the political system by granting corporations the right to spend unlimited amounts of money to influence elections. In 2010, half of the $300 million spent on political campaigns came from anonymous super PAC donors to create negative ads to oust those whose votes might threaten corporate profits. This distorts democracy and downplays the speech of those who oppose corporate interests. Since Congress is unlikely to act under the threat of super PAC campaign spending, a constitutional amendment is necessary to return to rule by the people for the people.*

If you are concerned about the collapse of the middle class, you should be concerned about how American campaigns are financed. If you wonder why the United States is the only country in the industrialized world not to have a national health care program, if you're asking why we pay the highest price in the world for prescription drugs, or why we spend more money on the military than the rest of the world combined, you are talking about campaign finance. You are talking about the unbelievable power that big-money interests have over every legislative decision.

Lowering the Floodgates

An already horrendous situation was made much worse two years ago this month [January 2010] when the Supreme Court ruled in *Citizens United v. the Federal Election Commission* that multinational corporations have a constitutional right to spend whatever they want to influence election outcomes. A bare 5–4 majority lowered the floodgates on unchecked, unlimited, unaccountable corporate cash in political campaigns. Corporations were equated with people. A century of laws regulating business spending on elections were upended. In one fell swoop, five justices fantasized for corporations a right never conceived by the founders whose preamble to our Constitution begins with the words, "We the people . . ."

The ruling not only poisoned our political process. It contaminated the legislative process. It cast a permanent chill over all policymaking. Will the merits or the money tip the balance when an issue comes before Congress? What do you think? If the question is on breaking up huge banks, for example, every member of the Senate and the House, in the back of their minds, will ask themselves what the personal price would be for taking on Wall Street. Am I going to be punished? Will a huge amount of money be unleashed in my state? They're going to think twice about how to cast that vote. Not to put too fine a point on it, you will see politicians being adopted by corporations and becoming wholly owned subsidiaries of corporate entities.

We already have seen what kind of damage *Citizens United* can cause. In the first election after the decision was handed down, corporations in 2010 poured hundreds of millions of dollars into independent organizations not formally affiliated with parties or candidates. About half of the $300 million spent by independent organizations came from undisclosed sources. In 60 of the 75 congressional races in which power changed hands, the unaccountable outside groups backed the winners. They spent freely and overwhelmingly on negative ads. The early phases of this year's elections bear witness to projections that the *Citizens United* effect will be much worse. Karl Rove [Republican political consultant] has announced plans to raise $240 million. The Koch brothers [conservative industrialists] promise to spend $200 million. It's fair to assume the Chamber of Commerce will spend at least as much. The Super PAC supporting President [Barack] Obama, Priorities USA Action, aims to play in the same league. Hundreds of millions more will be in play.

[A proposed constitutional] amendment would establish that constitutional rights belong to real people, not for-profit corporations.

Distorting Our Democracy

It's a virtual certainty that all of this spending will fundamentally distort our democracy, tilting the playing field to favor corporate interests, discouraging new candidates, chilling elected officials and shifting the overall policymaking debate even further in the direction of giant corporate interests and the super-wealthy.

So now we face a choice. Americans can let *Citizens United* remain the law of the land, or we can have a functioning democracy. We can't have both. We choose democracy. With no reason to think that this court will reconsider its decision, we need a constitutional amendment.

Yes, legislative reforms could mitigate the damage. We should require better disclosure rules. We should make shareholders approve corporations' political spending. We should provide public financing of elections, but entrenched money interests have thwarted that for decades.

But nothing can truly cure the problem unless *Citizens United* is overturned with a constitutional amendment.

The Saving American Democracy Amendment in the Senate and a companion proposed in the House by Florida Representative Ted Deutch would do just that. The amendment would establish that constitutional rights belong to real people, not for-profit corporations. The amendment would prohibit corporations from making election-related expenditures. It would clarify that Congress and states have the power to regulate campaign spending, overturning the doctrine that election contributions and expenditures constitute First Amendment-protected speech and therefore may be subject only to limited restrictions. And it would affirm that nothing in the amendment limits freedom of press.

It's no easy thing to enact a constitutional amendment, but momentum for an amendment is building. People who have honest differences of opinion understand that there is something profoundly disgusting with what is happening in Washington and that there is something wrong with American democracy when you have a handful of billionaires and businesses putting hundreds of millions of dollars into the political process. Very few people think that has anything to do with American democracy. The American people desperately want to restore our democracy and return to rule by all of the people, not corporations and the superrich.

12

Less Regulation of Campaigns Will Reduce the Role of Money in Politics

Ilya Shapiro

Ilya Shapiro is a senior fellow in constitutional studies at the Cato Institute, a libertarian think tank, and editor-in-chief of the Cato Supreme Court Review.

Eliminating restrictions on all forms of campaign spending will increase political speech and reduce potential political corruption. The Citizens United *Supreme Court decision, which removes restrictions on the political spending of corporations, unions, and other groups, increases their political speech. This creates an imbalance between independent and candidate spending. Prior to the* Citizens United *decision, campaign spending limits pushed money away from political candidates and toward advocacy groups. However, the solution is not to restrict the spending of these groups—people do not sacrifice rights by associating, whether as a union, a club, or for-profit business. The way to truly level the playing field is to remove all restrictions on campaign spending. Removing all limits and requiring disclosure would allow voters to interpret why an individual, a group, or a corporation is spending money in a political campaign.*

*C*itizens United is one of the most misunderstood Supreme Court decisions ever. It doesn't stand for what many people say it does.

Ilya Shapiro, "*Citizens United* and the 2012 Campaign," *Illinois Business Journal*, October 2012. Copyright © 2012 by Ilya Shapiro. All rights reserved. Reproduced by permission.

Take, for example, President [Barack] Obama's famous statement that the decision "reversed a century of law that I believe will open the floodgates for special interests—including foreign corporations—to spend without limit in our elections." In one sentence, the former law professor made four errors of law.

Understanding *Citizens United*

First, *Citizens United* didn't reverse a century of law. The president was referring to the Tillman Act of 1907, which prohibited corporate donations to candidates and parties. *Citizens United* didn't touch that. Instead, the overturned precedent was a 1990 case that, for the first and only time, allowed a restriction on political speech based on something other than the appearance of corruption.

The solution is obvious: Liberalize rather than restrict the [campaign finance] system.

Second, the "floodgates" point depends upon how you define those terms. As even the July 22 [2012] *New York Times* magazine reported, there's no significant change in corporate spending this cycle. There are certainly people running Super PACs [political action committees] who would otherwise be supporting candidates direct, but *Citizens United* didn't cause Super PACs (as I'll explain shortly). And the rules affecting the wealthy individuals who are spending more haven't changed at all. It's unclear that any "floodgates" have opened or which special interests didn't exist before.

The solution is obvious: Liberalize rather than restrict the system.

Third, the rights of foreigners—corporate or otherwise—is another issue about which *Citizens United* said nothing. Indeed, just this year, the Supreme Court summarily upheld the restriction on foreign spending in political campaigns.

Fourth and finally, while independent spending on elections now has few limits, candidates and parties aren't so lucky, and neither are their donors. Again, *Citizens United* didn't affect laws regarding individual or corporate contributions to candidates.

Allowing Smaller Players to Speak

More important than *Citizens United* was *SpeechNow.org v. FEC [Federal Election Commission]*, decided two months later [March 26, 2010] in the D.C. Circuit. That ruling removed limits on donations to political action committees, thus making these PACs "super" and freeing people to pool money the same way one rich person can alone.

> *The underlying problem . . . isn't the under-regulation of independent [campaign] spending but the attempt to manage political speech in the first place.*

And so, if you're concerned about the money spent on elections—though Americans spend more on chewing gum and Easter candy—the problem isn't with big corporate players. That is another misapprehension: Exxon, Halliburton and all these "evil" companies (or even the good ones) are not suddenly dominating the political conversation. They spend little money on political advertising, partly because it's more effective to lobby, but mostly because they wouldn't want to alienate half their customers. As [superstar athlete] Michael Jordan famously said, "Republicans buy shoes, too."

On the other hand, groups composed of individuals and smaller players now get to speak: Your National Federation of Independent Business and Sierra Clubs, your ACLUs [American Civil Liberties Union] and Planned Parenthoods. So even if we accept "leveling the playing field" as a proper basis for regulation, the freeing of associational speech levels that field.

Moreover, people don't lose rights when they get together, be it in unions, advocacy groups, clubs, for-profit companies or any other way.

Nevertheless, various bills and constitutional amendments have been proposed to remedy some of *Citizens United*'s perceived ills. The idea behind these efforts is that elections will be cleaner if we can only eliminate private campaign money.

Managing Political Speech

The underlying problem, however, isn't the under-regulation of independent spending but the attempt to manage political speech in the first place. Political money is like water: it'll flow somewhere because what government does matters and people want to speak about their concerns. To the extent that "money in politics" is a problem, the solution is to reduce the political scope that money can influence. Shrink government, and you'll shrink the amount people spend trying to get a piece of the pie.

While we await that shrinkage, we do have to address the core flaw in the campaign finance regime. That original sin was committed by the Supreme Court, not in *Citizens United*, but in the 1976 *Buckley v. Valeo*. By rewriting the Watergate-era Federal Election Campaign Act to remove spending limits but not contribution caps, *Buckley* upset Congress's balance reform.[1]

That's why politicians spend all their time fundraising. Moreover, the regulations have pushed money away from candidates and toward advocacy groups, undermining the worthy goal of government accountability.

The solution is obvious: Liberalize rather than restrict the system. Get rid of limits on individual contributions, and then require disclosures for those who donate amounts big enough

---

1. Watergate was a political scandal wherein a break-in occurred at the Democratic National Committee, and the administration of President Richard Nixon attempted to cover up its involvement.

for the interest in preventing corruption to outweigh the potential harassment. Then the big boys will have to put their reputations on the line, but not the average person. Let voters weigh what a donation's source means to them, rather than allowing politicians to write rules benefiting themselves.

An Unbalanced System

We no[w] have a system that's unbalanced and unworkable. At some point, however, there will be enough incumbents who feel that they're losing message control to such an extent that they'll allow fairer political markets. Earlier this summer, for example, the Democratic governor of Illinois signed a law allowing unlimited contributions in races with significant independent spending. This deregulation is an act of political self-preservation, but that's fine.

The way to 'take back our democracy' . . . isn't to further restrict political speech but rethink the basic premise of existing regulations.

Once more politicians realize that they can't prevent communities from organizing, they'll want to capture more of their dollars. Stephen Colbert would then have to focus on other laws to lampoon, but I'm confident that he can do that and we'll be better off on all counts.[2]

Ultimately, the way to "take back our democracy"—to invoke the name of the campaign-finance hearing at which I re-

2. Stephen Colbert, who portrays himself as a conservative political pundit in a political television talk show parody, created his own super PAC to draw public attention to the influence of super PACs. He named the organization Americans for a Better Tomorrow, Tomorrow. Speaking in character, Colbert said the money would be raised not only for political ads, but also "normal administrative expenses, including but not limited to, luxury hotel stays, private jet travel, and PAC mementos from Saks Fifth Avenue and Neiman Marcus." Colbert received a Peabody Award for his "innovative means of teaching American viewers about the landmark court decision" that led to the rise of super PACs.

cently testified—isn't to further restrict political speech but to rethink the basic premise of existing regulations.

13

Protect Democracy from Corporate Cash Tsunami

Clara Torres-Spelliscy

Clara Torres-Spelliscy, an assistant professor at Stetson University College of Law, in Gulfport, Florida, is co-author with Kathy Fogel of "Shareholder-Authorized Corporate Political Spending in the United Kingdom," published in the University of San Francisco Law Review.

If corporations may, through super political action committees (PACs), engage in unlimited political spending independent of campaigns, governments need to establish rules to make the process transparent to shareholders and investors. The United Kingdom, for example, requires that public companies report all political spending and that investors vote whether companies may spend money on politics. While waiting for long-term action, federal rules might come from the Securities and Exchange Commission (SEC), an idea popular among the public. Some states have already begun to act so that voters know the source of political spending. Ultimately, Congress should enact a Shareholder Protection Act that requires disclosure and consent. If corporations are going to participate in the election process, voters, shareholders, and investors need to know.

Lost in the hubbub about health care, the Supreme Court reaffirmed its unpopular *Citizens United* decision, blithely stripping Montana of a century old law that protected its elections from corporate politicking.[1] In summarily reversing Montana's highest court, the Supreme Court [on June 25, 2012] decided the state wouldn't even get the opportunity to present its case, leaving voters nationwide having to deal with the results of virtually unlimited cash in elections.

So now what?

For one thing, with corporations in our elections to stay, we need some new rules of the road that are tailored for corporations.

First, there should be clear disclosure to investors that the [campaign] spending is happening. Second, there should be a way for investors to approve the political expenditures.

If I'm donating to a campaign, then I am spending my own money. This is not the same as a CEO [chief executive officer] at a public company buying political ads with corporate resources. In that case, the CEO is using what Supreme Court Justice Louis Brandeis once termed "other people's money."

Investor Consent

The other people in this case include investors, who may have no interest in subsidizing a CEO's pet political projects or disagree about what government policies are best for the com-

---

1. The author refers to Montana's Corrupt Practices Act, enacted in 1912. The conservative political action committee (PAC) American Tradition Partnership (ATP) challenged the law, which prohibited corporate campaign spending when the Montana Commission of Political Practices ruled that ATP had broken state campaign laws. The state's Supreme Court upheld the law. However, the US Supreme Court ordered that Montana stop enforcing it pending its own review of whether it violates federal mandate. According to Steve Bullock, Montana's attorney general, states "should have the right to be the masters of their own elections" because "the integrity of our system and the voices of Montanans, whatever their political views, are too important to be drowned out by modern-day copper kings." Nevertheless, citing *Citizens United*, the US Supreme court overturned the Montana law.

pany. Thus, there should be different rules that apply when insiders spend other people's money in politics.

What would these different rules look like? First, there should be clear disclosure to investors that the spending is happening. Second, there should be a way for investors to approve the political expenditures.

The United Kingdom [U.K.] is showing the way. Public companies report political spending down to the pound to investors, and investors get to vote on the political budgets of the companies before they spend the money in politics.

At the federal level, new rules could come from the Securities and Exchange Commission [SEC] so that investors can one-stop shop for comprehensive company-specific reports. A group of professors has already asked the SEC for a transparency rule. So far, a record-breaking 300,000 members of the public have commented and asked the SEC to act.

The only thing worse than a corporation trying to buy an election is one that gets to do so covertly without even letting its shareholders in on the secret.

Longer-term solutions for federal elections include the Shareholder Protection Act, which has been introduced in Congress and would provide the same transparency and consent for shareholders enjoyed by U.K. investors for more than a decade.

State Initiatives

Although the federal DISCLOSE Act [Democracy Is Strengthened by Casting Light on Spending in Elections] was shot down in the Senate this week [July 2012], states can amend their elections laws to give voters greater clarity about exactly who is trying to influence their vote. According to a June [2012] report from the Corporate Reform Coalition, 17 states—including key battle grounds Colorado, Wisconsin and

Florida—already have strong laws providing transparency in state and local elections that will contrast strongly with the dearth of information available about corporate spending in those same states' federal elections. Thirteen states have weak laws that mostly leave voters in the dark, among them Ohio and New Mexico.

In addition, states could adopt their own laws that require board approval or shareholder consent for corporations. Missouri, Louisiana and Iowa require board approval of corporate political spending. Maryland requires corporate political expenditures to be reported to shareholders. And bills to empower shareholders with a "say on politics" vote have been introduced in six states.

Corporations are going to be in elections, and we need to cope with that fact. The only thing worse than a corporation trying to buy an election is one that gets to do so covertly without even letting its shareholders in on the secret.

Organizations to Contact

The editors have compiled the following list of organizations concerned with the issues debated in this book. The descriptions are derived from materials provided by the organizations. All have publications or information available for interested readers. The list was compiled on the date of publication of the present volume; names, addresses, phone and fax numbers, and e-mail and Internet addresses may change. Be aware that many organizations take several weeks or longer to respond to inquiries, so allow as much time as possible.

American Enterprise Institute for Public Policy Research (AEI)
1150 Seventeenth St. NW, Washington, DC   20036
(202) 862-5800 • fax: (202) 862-7177
website: www.aei.org

AEI is a conservative think tank based in Washington, DC. Its scholars support campaign reforms that would eliminate spending restrictions on political parties that would allow challengers to compete with incumbents. AEI publishes articles and commentary by AEI scholars on issues concerning campaign finance and other issues related to political campaigns on its website, including "Reform in an Age of Networked Campaigns" and "Super PACS Engage in More Positive Than Negative Messaging."

Brennan Center for Justice at New York University School of Law
161 Ave. of the Americas, 12th Floor, New York, NY   10013
(212) 998-6730 • fax: (212) 995-4550
e-mail: brennancenter@nyu.edu
website: www.brennancenter.org

The Brennan Center for Justice at New York University School of Law is a non-partisan public policy and law institute that focuses on fundamental issues of democracy and justice. One part of the center's work involves advocacy for voting rights and federal election reform. The group tracks election reform activity at the federal level, including legislation, news, and research. The website includes links to news articles, reports, and other publications, including "Americans Hate Super PACs. But Will They Vote Against Them?" and "Undoing the Damage of *Citizens United.*"

Brookings Institution
1775 Massachusetts Ave. NW, Washington, DC   20036
(202) 797-6000 • fax: (202) 797-6004
e-mail: communications@brookings.edu
website: www.brookings.edu

Founded in 1927, the Brookings Institution conducts research and analyzes global events and their impact on the United States and US foreign policy. It publishes the *Brookings Review* quarterly as well as numerous books and research papers. Resources on super PACS and campaign finance can be found through its campaign finance link or the institute's search engine, including the live events, "Political Voice and American Democracy: Unequal and Undemocratic" and "Campaign Finance in the 2012 Elections. The Rise of the Super PACs," and the Brookings expert blog commentary "Killing Public Discourse in Campaign Finance."

Campaign Finance Institute (CFI)
1425 K St. NW, Suite 350, Washington, DC   20005
(202) 969-8890 • fax: (202) 969 5612
e-mail: info@cfinst.org
website: www.cfinst.org

Founded in 1999, CFI is a nonprofit and non-partisan campaign finance think tank that develops reports and makes recommendations for government officials and the general public. CFI also tracks spending and fundraising by candidates and interest groups. The majority of CFI's publications are free and available for download from the institute's website.

Articles on the campaign finance of special interest groups and super PACS are available on its Interest Groups link, including the presentation "PACs in an Age of Super PACs."

Cato Institute

1000 Massachusetts Ave. NW, Washington, DC   20001-5403
(202) 842-0200 • fax: (202) 842-3490
website: www.cato.org

The Cato Institute is a libertarian public policy research foundation dedicated to limited government and support of the free market. It generally opposes any campaign finance restrictions. It publishes numerous reports, analysis, commentary, and the periodicals, *Policy Analysis* and *Cato Policy Review*. Resources on campaign finance and super PACs are available on its website, including "Are Super PACs Good for Democracy?" and "Meet the Parents of the Super PACs."

Center for Competitive Politics (CCP)

901 N Glebe Rd., Suite 900, Arlington, VA   22203
(703) 682-9359 • fax: (703) 682-9321
e-mail: info@campaignfreedom.org
website: www.campaignfreedom.org

The CCP was founded as a nonprofit organization in 2005 by former Federal Elections Commission Chairman Bradley A. Smith. The center seeks to promote a more fair and open electoral process. CCP publishes legal briefs, reports, and studies on the issue. Members of the center often testify before Congress and other public bodies and transcripts of their presentations, as well as other documents on the *Citizens United* decision and super PACs, can be found on its website, including "Spending and Amending: The Past and Future of *Citizens United*" and "So What if Corporations Aren't People?"

Center for Responsive Politics (CRP)

1011 14th St. NW, Suite 10300, Washington, DC   20005
(202) 857-0044 • fax: (202) 857-7809

e-mail: info@crp.org
website: www.opensecrets.org

CRP is an independent nonprofit organization that aims to create a more educated voter, an involved citizenry, and a more transparent and responsive government. Through its website, OpenSecrets.org, the center informs citizens about how money in politics affects their lives, empowers voters and activists by providing unbiased information, and advocates for a transparent and responsive government. The website provides resources on federal campaign contributions and tracks money in politics, including super PACs.

Democracy 21
2000 Massachusetts Ave. NW, Washington, DC   20036
(202) 355-9600
e-mail: info@democracy21.org
website: www.democracy21.org

Democracy 21 is a nonpartisan advocacy group that works to eliminate the undue influence of big money in American politics, prevent government corruption, empower citizens in the political process, and ensure the integrity and fairness of government decisions and elections. The organization promotes campaign finance reform and other related political reforms to accomplish these goals. On its website Democracy 21 publishes letters to Congress and the Federal Elections Commission as well as articles on *Citizens United*, including "Election Is Over, but 'Super PACs' Remain a Threat," "The Power of Anonymity," and "Disclosure Democracy."

Democratic National Committee (DNC)
430 S Capitol St. SE, Washington, DC   20003
(202) 863-8000
website: www.democrats.org

The DNC is the governing body of the Democratic party in the United States. The partisan organization provides information on major national and state issues it believes of concern to voters. It also offers details on how to get involved in political campaigns. The DNC provides information on Democratic candidates and campaign events. Its website examines contemporary legislation and legal issues from a Democratic perspective and provides details about the party organization and structure.

Federal Election Commission (FEC)
999 E St. NW, Washington, DC   20463
(800) 424-9530
website: www.fec.gov

Congress created the FEC as an independent regulatory agency in 1975 to administer and enforce the Federal Election Campaign Act (FECA)—the statute that governs the financing of federal elections. The duties of the FEC are to disclose campaign finance information, to enforce the provisions of the law such as the limits and prohibitions on contributions, and to oversee the public funding of presidential elections. The website provides useful information about campaign finance issues and the laws and regulations governing this matter.

Public Campaign
1133 19th St. NW, 9th Floor, Washington, DC   20036
(202) 640-56000 • fax: (202) 640-6501
e-mail: info@publicampaign.org
website: www.publicampaign.org

Public Campaign is a nonpartisan campaign finance reform organization that seeks to reduce the role of special interest money in American politics. On its website the campaign publishes educational materials on various campaign reform measures and provides news, polling data, and commentary on money in politics.

Reason Foundation
3415 S Sepulveda Blvd., Suite 400, Los Angeles, CA   90034
(310) 391-2245 • fax: (310) 391-4395
website: www.reason.org

The Reason Foundation promotes individual freedoms and free-market principles, and opposes campaign finance restrictions. On its website, the foundation publishes newsletters, testimony, court briefs, policy studies, and commentary by foundation policy experts and articles from the monthly *Reason* magazine, including "Why Super PACs Are Good for Democracy."

Republican National Committee (RNC)
310 1st St. SE, Washington, DC   20003
(202) 863-8500
website: www.gop.com

The RNC is the governing body of the Republican party, also known as the Grand Old Party. This partisan political group offers details on significant national and state issues and information on political involvement and voter guides. The RNC presents information on Republican candidates, primaries, and campaign events. Its website analyzes issues from a Republican perspective and provides an overview of the party's organization and structure.

Bibliography

Books

Floyd Abrams   *Friend of the Court: On the Front Lines with the First Amendment*. New Haven, CT: Yale University Press, 2013.

Michael Barone and Chuck McCutcheon   *The Almanac of American Politics 2012*. Chicago, IL: The University of Chicago Press, 2011.

William L. Benoit   *Communication in Political Campaigns*. New York: Peter Lang, 2007.

John Bicknell and David Meyers, eds.   *Politics in America 2012: 112th Congress*. Washington, DC: CQ Roll Call, 2011.

Jeffrey D. Clement   *Corporations Are Not People: Why They Have More Rights than You Do and What You Can Do About It*. San Francisco, CA: Berrett-Koehler, 2012.

Victoria A. Farrar-Myers and Diana Dwyre   *Limits & Loopholes: The Quest for Money, Free Speech, and Fair Elections*, Washington, DC: CQ Press, 2008.

Lawrence Lessig   *Republic, Lost: How Money Corrupts Congress—and a Plan to Stop It*. New York: Twelve, 2011.

John Nichols and Robert W. McChesney — *Dollarocracy: How the Money-and-Media Election Complex Is Destroying America*. New York: Nation Books, 2013.

Richard J. Semiatin, ed. — *Campaigns on the Cutting Edge*. Thousand Oaks, CA: CQ Press, 2013.

Melissa M. Smith, ed. — *Campaign Finance Reform: The Political Shell Game*. Lanham, MD: Rowman & Littlefield, 2010.

Monica Youn — *Money, Politics, and the Constitution: Beyond Citizens United*. New York: The Century Foundation, 2011.

Periodicals and Internet Sources

Steven J. Andre — "The Transformation of Freedom of Speech: Unsnarling the Twisted Roots of *Citizens United v. FEC*," *John Marshall Law Review*, 2010.

John Avlon and Michael Keller — "The Super-PAC Economy," *Daily Beast*, September 18, 2012. www .thedailybeast.com.

Nick Baumann — "Grayson: Court's Campaign Finance Decision 'Worst Since Dred Scott,'" *Mother Jones*, January 22, 2010. www .motherjones.com.

Ari Berman — "The .000063% Election," *Huffington Post*, February 16, 2012. www .huffingtonpost.com.

John Blake — "Forgetting a Key Lesson from Watergate?" CNN.com, February 4, 2012.

Joan Biskupic   "Supreme Court Cases Test Speech Rights—and More," *USA Today*, March 30, 2010.

Josh Boak   "Enter the Era of Super PACs," *Campaign & Elections*, September 8, 2011.

Eliza Carney   "Court Unlikely to Stop with *Citizens United*," *National Journal*, January 21, 2010.

Nancy Cordes   "Colbert Gets a Super PAC; So What Are They?" CBS News, June 20, 2011.

Economist   "The Hands That Prod, the Wallets That Feed," February 25, 2012.

Peter Grier   "Will Jon Stewart Go to Jail for Running Stephen Colbert's Super PAC?" *Christian Science Monitor*, January 18, 2012.

Richard L. Hasen   "Money Grubbers: The Supreme Court Kills Campaign Finance Reform," *Slate*, January 21, 2010. www.slate.com.

Richard L. Hasen   "Occupy the Super PACs," *Slate*, February 20, 2012. www.slate.com.

Kenneth Jost   "Campaign Finance Debates," *CQ Researcher*, May 28, 2010.

Colbert I. King   "In D.C., a Mockery of Campaign Finance Laws," *Washington Post*, January 13, 2012.

Shannon McGovern   "Going Dirty," *US News Digital Weekly*, July 27, 2012. www.usnews .com/weekly.

Timothy Noah   "Crankocracy in America," *New Republic*, March 29, 2012.

Dave Nyczepir   "The Super PAC Onslaught: Is Your Local Campaign Next?" *Campaigns & Elections*, July/August 2012. www .campaignsandelections.com.

Jonathan Riskind   "The More Disclosure, the Better," *Columbus Dispatch*, February 7, 2010. www.dispatch.com.

Joel Seligman   "Is the Corporation the Person? Reflections on *Citizens United v. Federal Election Commission*," University of Rochester: Office of the President, May 6, 2010. www .rochester.edu.

Jim Sleeper   "Corporate Free Speech? Since When?" *Boston Globe*, September 5, 2009.

Rodney A. Smith   "High Court Aided Free Speech But Should Have Gone Further," *Washington Times*, February 17, 2010.

Seth Barrett Tillman   "*Citizens United* and the Scope of Professor Teachout's Anti-Corruption Principle," *Northwestern University Law Review Colloquy*, 2012.

Jeffrey Toobin   "Money Unlimited: How Chief Justice John Roberts Orchestrated the *Citizens United* Decision," *New Yorker*, May 21, 2012.

U.S. News & World Report   "Are Super PACs Harming US Politics?" Debate Club, January 13, 2012.

David Von Drehle   "Campaign Finance and the Court," *Time*, February 8, 2010.

Julian Zelizer   "It Took a Scandal to Get Real Campaign Finance Reform," CNN.com, January 23, 2012.

Index

A

Adelson, Sheldon, 22
Alito, Samuel, 26
Allison, Bill, 78
Allott, Gordon, 17
American Civil Liberties Union (ACLU), 10, 88
American Independent Business Alliance, 42
Americans for Prosperity, Workers' Voice, 7
American University, 41
America's Health Insurance Plans (AHIP), 27
Ansolabehere, Stephen, 21
Anthony, Susan B., 35, 44
Austin v. Michigan Chamber of Commerce (1990), 47
Avlon, John, 75–81
Axelrod, David, 13

B

Bachus, Spencer, 60
Bai, Matt, 11
Baran, Jan Witold, 10, 45–49
Bartels, Larry, 57
Bennet, Michael, 17
Boehner, John, 10
Bonifaz, John, 43, 44
Bowie, Blair, 50–58
Bradley, Bill, 18
Brookings Institution, 23
Brown, Sherrod, 38
Buck, Ken, 17

Buckley v. Valeo (1976), 7–8, 70, 89
Burrus, Trevor, 30–33

C

Campaign for Primary Accountability, 60
Campaign Legal Center, 8, 78–79
Cantwell, Maria, 79
Capitalism and role of money, 52–53
Carson, André, 40
Casting Light on Spending in Elections Act, 19
Castro, Fidel, 60
Center for Media and Democracy, 39, 42
Center for Responsive Politics, 26
Citizens United v. Federal Election Commission (2010)
    amendment to overturn needed, 82–85
    assault on super PACs with, 12–24
    controversy over, 71–73
    corporations and, 34–44
    defense of, 63–68
    distortion of democracy, 84–85
    flaws with, 69–74, 84
    impact of, 25–26, 47–48
    less campaign regulation needed, 86–91
    message to Congress over, 48–49
    overview, 8

At Issue

| Super PACs

Other Books in the At Issue Series: